THE GODS OF THE VIKINGS

Published by Avalonia

BM Avalonia
London
WC1N 3XX
England, UK

www.avaloniabooks.co.uk

The Gods of the Vikings
Copyright © Marion Pearce 2008

ISBN-10: 1-905297-44-0
ISBN-13: 978-1-905297-44-3

First Edition, November 2010

Illustrations © Emily Carding 2008

Design by Satori
Edited by D. Kennedy

Cover Art 'Odin' © Emily Carding 2008

British Library Cataloguing in Publication Data. A catalogue
record for this book is available from the British Library.

DEDICATION

This book is dedicated to my late husband Dave Pearce

ACKNOWLEDGEMENTS

I would like to thank and acknowledge Alan Nash of The Kith of Yggdrasil for his help, see The Kith of Yggdrasil website www.kithofyggdrasil.host56.com

THE GODS
OF THE
VIKINGS

EXPLORING THE NORSE GODS, MYTHS AND
LEGENDS THROUGH THE DAYS OF THE WEEK

BY MARION PEARCE

ILLUSTRATED BY EMILY CARDING

PUBLISHED BY AVALONIA
WWW.AVALONIABOOKS.CO.UK

ABOUT THE AUTHOR

MARION PEARCE

Marion Pearce is the author of several books and articles on Celtic, Norse and Roman history and culture. Her work has been published in magazines in the UK and internationally. She is the editor of *Pentacle Magazine*, the biggest independent pagan magazine in the UK, which she founded in 2002; and was formerly the editor of *Pagan Dawn*, the magazine of the Pagan Federation.

Marion is the author of several books including:
> *Celts: Masters of Fire* (2008, with Poppy Palin) Capall Bann, Chieveley
> *Origins and Festivals of the Roman Calendar* (2004) Capall Bann, Chieveley
> *Celtic Sacrifice: Pre-Christian Ritual and Religion* (2001) Capall Bann, Chievely
> *Milton, Chalkwell and the Crowstone* (2000), Ian Henry, Essex

You can write to the author:
Marion Pearce, c/o Avalonia, BM Avalonia, London, WC1N 3XX, England, UK

TABLE OF CONTENTS

Introduction..10

Part 1 The Days of the Week................................. 13
    Days and the Week 15
    The Naming of the Days 21

Part 2 Anglo-Saxon, Norse & Christian Worldviews25
    The Anglo-Saxon World in the Age of the Vikings.. 27
    Norse Paganism and Christianity 47

Part 3 Beginnings and Endings 75
    The Norse Story of Creation 77
    Norse Cosmology and the Lands of Death............. 96
    Ragnarok the Norse End of the World...................108

**Part 4 The Norse Gods and Myths expressed through
the Days of the Week** 121
    Sunday..123
    Monday 133
    Tuesday...140
    Wednesday 147
    Thursday 161
    Friday...176
    Saturday 188

Appendix 197
    Pagan Saxon/Norse Festivals 198
    May Day 202
    Summer Solstice...207
    Yule...210

Bibliography 213
Index 219

ABOUT THE ARTIST

EMILY CARDING

Emily Carding is a self-taught artist and author, as well as a Priestess, lyricist, actor, singer, and mother. Her inspiration comes from vibrant mythology in all cultures and reality in magic and the Otherworld.

Her published work includes:
> *The Transparent Tarot* (2008), Schiffer Publishing Ltd, Pennsylvania
> *The Transparent Oracle* (2010), Schiffer Publishing Ltd, Pennsylvania
> *The Tarot of the Sidhe* (2011), Schiffer Publishing Ltd, Pennsylvania

She has also contributed essays to the following anthologies:
> *Hekate Her Sacred Fires* (2010), Avalonia, London
> *From a Drop of Water* (2009), Avalonia, London
> *Both Sides of Heaven* (2009), Avalonia, London

You can write to the artist:
Emily Carding, c/o Avalonia, BM Avalonia, London, WC1N 3XX, England, UK

Or visit her website: www.childofavalon.com

LIST OF ILLUSTRATIONS

Figure 1 - Beowulf..31
Figure 2 - Dragon Guardian 33
Figure 3 - Temple...50
Figure 4 - Yggdrasil..59
Figure 5 - Valhalla's Gate 61
Figure 6 - Ymir..84
Figure 7 - Skoll & Hati 87
Figure 8 - Alfheim 89
Figure 9 - Heimdall 93
Figure 10 - Svartalfheim 97
Figure 11 - Valkyrie 100
Figure 12 - Hel..103
Figure 13 - Loki's Children..106
Figure 14 - Ragnarok 109
Figure 15 - Baldur's Brow 128
Figure 16 - Tyr...143
Figure 17 - Hugin and Munin..................................152
Figure 18 - Odin's Sacrifice 158
Figure 19 - Thor..166
Figure 20 - Sif...169
Figure 21 - Longship...173
Figure 22 – Frigg...179
Figure 23 - Freya 185
Figure 24 - Loki 192
Figure 25 - The Norns 195

INTRODUCTION

The days of the week. They are in use all the time, but how did they get their names? There is more to them than meets the eye. Each day represented a Saxon and Norse, Viking god. These gods were sacred. Through the days of the week you can reconstruct the ancient religion of the Saxons and Norse and their world.

Before we can understand them it is interesting to look further into the world of the Northmen, who are perhaps better known as Vikings. The word Viking itself means 'bay-men' or 'fighting men'. It's a collective term referring to the Danes, Norwegians and Swedes. For the sake of clarity I have interchanged the terms Danes, Norse, Northmen and Viking.

This was a totally different world to the modern one of today. The Vikings plundered, raped and pillaged their way through Anglo-Saxon Britain bringing fear and terror to the hearts of the inhabitants. But they also brought with them their religion, so totally different from that of Christianity.

Britain had been converted from the Anglo-Saxon pagan religion by Pope Gregory when he sent Saint Augustine together with thirty monks to evangelise the Anglo-Saxons of England. Augustine landed in Ebbsfleet in Kent in 597 CE. Christianity was on its way.

The country remained Christian till the Vikings raided Lindisfarne in Northumbria on the 8th of January 793 CE. England would not be the same again. The dreaded aggressive Vikings had arrived, ravaging their way through the land and causing destruction whereever they went.

The fearsome Vikings brought with them their own beliefs, utterly alien to the British. This was a warlike religion, suited to the hard terrain of Iceland from where it originated. Life in Iceland was hard with the land inhospitable. The climate made it hard to live there with its short summers and long cold winters. There were glaciers and frosts. These and the harsh frequent storms were attributed to the power of the equally harsh gods.

For the Vikings to exist they had to rely on the spoils of other countries which they could raid. Unfortunately for those raided, their methods were severe. The murder of men women and children and the rape of females that they encountered were widespread. In fact massacres of whole communities were common. Those were frightening days.

But to understand them more fully you have to look deeper into the world of the Anglo-Saxon and that of the Norse; to look into the Norse religion, which is very different to that of the modern Christian world.

Let's pull back the mists of time and explore this ancient world so different from that of now. By exploring the meaning of each day and comparing it to the remarkable race of people who named the days of the week we can build a picture of how our weekly calendar grew to its present form.

PART 1
THE DAYS OF THE WEEK

DAYS AND THE WEEK

It has been observed that *"the year is timed by nature, the unequal lengths of the months by tradition and the week by authority."*[1] However the week was not always divided by seven days. Different cultures had different time units dividing their week. There were three, five as well as seven day weeks among ancient societies.

Both the Romans and the Etruscans used the market week of eight days. To the Romans this was seven days of work, plus an extra day known as the *'nundinae'*. The Nundinae was the day for the market. The rural population flocked to the market in the town. The day became a day of festivity, public auctions were held. It was a day of rest.

When the week was altered to its present seven day form the last day was still left as a special holiday for rest, celebration and jubilation. Flavius Josephus (37-c.100 CE) the noted Jewish historian commentated that by the end of the first century:

> *"There is no city, Greek or barbarian, not a people, to whom our custom of abstaining from work on the seventh day has not spread."*[2]

Thus the custom of the Sabbath was born, from earlier Pagan celebrations. This concept of a day of rest became very important in the Judeo-Christian world. The word Sabbath comes from the Hebrew *sabbat* meaning *'to rest'*. This is reflected in the *Bible*:

> *"And on the seventh day God ended his work which he had made; and he rested on the seventh day from all his work which he had made.*
> *And God blessed the seventh day, and sanctified it: because that in it he had rested from all his work which God created and made."*[3]

---

[1] Marking Time, Steel, 1999:86.
[2] Against Apion 2,40, Josephus, c.97 CE.
[3] Genesis 2:2-3.

The Sabbath is still very important indeed to both the Christian and Jewish faiths, although to Christianity it is held on Sunday, and to the Jewish world it starts on Friday night at sunset, continuing through to sunset on Saturday. It is now though considered a day for prayer as well as rest. The term Sabbath was commonly used instead of Sunday until the 17th Century.

Sabbaths were also totally different to various religions. Each had their own unique day. Here is a verse describing those Sabbaths according to each belief system:

> "Christians worship god on Sunday,
> Grecian zealots hallow Monday,
> Tuesday Persians spend in prayer,
> Assyrians Wednesday revere,
> Egyptians Thursday,
> Friday Turks,
> On Saturday no Hebrew works."[4]

According to different civilisation the day starts at different times. For many cultures the day started at sunset on the previous day. This is normal in the Jewish Faith and some Christian festivals begin on the eve of the preceding day. This was also common to the ancient Britons, the Athenians, the Chinese, the Germans and the Gauls.

In other cultures the day commenced at sunrise. These were the beliefs of the Babylonians, the Syrians, and the Persians. The ancient Egyptians believed the day started at noon. Only our modern world has the day begin at midnight. The beginning of the day depended on where you lived and what culture was prevalent.

How days were counted was different as well. Both the Celts and the Germans counted their days by 'nights', whereas according to Homer the ancient Greeks numbered their time by 'dawns'.

To ancient cultures only the period of daylight mattered. That was when you could work, the hours of night and darkness were not important. In the days before artificial lighting, the time when the main light was that of the moon, then it was difficult to labour. There was insufficient light. Although there were candles and basic lamp these forms of

---

[4] Brewer's Dictionary of Phrase and Fable, Brewer, 1898.

lighting were expensive and lacking in illumination. In fact the early Greek, and Latin word *dies*, for *day*, had two meanings. One was for the time from the sun's rising to its setting. The other definition was that of a full day, from the sun's rising to its rising again the next day. Thus in most civilisations the day was considered to start in the morning.

The days were not always divided into hours. Time was not as exact as it is today. But during times of war some means was needed to separate the day. A system of watches was used. The *Old Testament* and Homer used three watches during the day and three during the night. The Egyptians and later the Greeks and Romans used four watches to measure their day. Although some early societies used the simpler system of two watches, one for the day and one for the night.

The Babylonian civilisation, in what is now Iraq had an interesting version of their calendar. It was a lunar calendar that started with the new moon and consisted of twelve months divided into twenty-nine and thirty days in turn. In this way they had a lunar year which really only consisted of 354 days divided into six summer months (April-October) and six winter months (October-April).This was compensated for by adding an extra leap month so that the new year would always start at the same point of time. This way the Babylonians got rid of the wandering year and had a calendar year which actually was in accordance with the real solar year.

From Babylon originates the division of day and night into equally long hours which were divided into two halves, the day-watch and the night-watch. Thus they got the sacred cosmic number of 12, which was the foundation of the Babylonian numerical system which used the number 60 as a base. This was a positional system (the so-called sexagesimal system) which made it possible to divide up hours into both degrees of angle and minutes and then minutes into sixty seconds.

The Egyptians first divided the days into hours in 2100 BCE. There was a system of twenty four hours used by the priesthood. This arrangement was separated into ten daylight hours, two twilight hours and twelve night hours. This was simplified in 1300 BCE to a system of twelve hours to the day and another twelve hours for the night time. This last method was used by the Babylonians and the Greeks who learnt it from the Babylonians.

From a very early time, the ancient Egyptians had a form of calendar based upon the phases of the moon that followed a calendar system of 360 days, with three seasons, each made up of 4 months, with thirty days in each month. The seasons of the Egyptians corresponded with the cycles of the Nile, and were known as Inundation (*akhet* which lasted from June 21st to October 21st), Emergence (*proyet* which lasted from October 21st to February 21st), and Low-water or Harvest (*shomu* which lasted from February 21st to June 21st).

The beginning of the year, also called *'the opening of the year'*, was marked by the emergence of the star Sirius, in the constellation of Canis Major. The constellation emerged roughly on June 21st, and was called *'the going up of the goddess Sothis'*. The star was visible just before sunrise, and is still one of the brightest stars in the sky, located to the lower left of Orion and taking the form of the dogs nose in the constellation Canis Major.

Though the Egyptians did have a 360 day calendar, in a literal sense they did have a 365 day calendar system. The beginning of the year was marked by the addition of five additional days, known as *'the yearly five days'*. These additional five days, were times of great feasting and celebration for the Egyptians, and it was not uncommon for the Egyptians to rituals and other celebratory dealings on these days. As they made no provision for a leap year, the calendar and the seasons drifted out of step, and by the end of the Old Kingdom there was a discrepancy of five months.

The actual word *hour* comes from the Latin *'hora'*. But the word originally meant season. This was later amended to an appointed time. In fact one of the earliest references to the hour was for a lovers' assignation.

The first hour as we know it today appeared during the second half of the fourth century BCE, when the term half hour also emerged.

The hours were calculated from either the rising of the sun or at night from the beginning of darkness. So the seventh hour would be roughly the same as the modern midday, being counted from the dawn. This would have signalled the end of business hours. By the same token, the ninth hour would have been the equivalent of approx. 1.30pm to 2.30pm or dinner time in imperial Rome.

Early civilisations calculated time from the sun during the day, and the stars during the night. Time was measured from the length of a man's shadow. Primitive tables have been found showing the connection between the human shadow and the seasonal hour of the day. During the night the Egyptian priests used a star clock to measure time by the sky. This form of clock was known as early as 1800 BCE.

The next developments in the counting of time were the water clock and the sun dial. The earliest preserved water clock dates from 1600 BCE and the sun dial from 1450 BCE. Both of these instruments were found in Egypt which appears to have been quite advanced when it comes to telling the time. Evidently according to the Greek chronicler, Herodotus c. 484-425 BCE, the Greeks learnt the art of the sun dial from the Babylonians. Although there is a tradition that the first Greek sundial was constructed by either the philosopher Anaximander of Miletus, c. 610-540 BCE or his student, Anaximenes of Miletus, c. 546 BCE.

These two philosophers were very important to the understanding of time. Anaximander was an astronomer. He believed that the planets circled the earth. This theory was in use until Copernicus (1473–1543 CE) made the revolutionary discovery that it was sun that the planets orbited, not the earth. The ancient Greek, Anaximander, (c. 610 - 546 BCE) was a pre-Socratic Greek philosopher who lived in Miletus, a city of Ionia (now called Milet in modern Turkey). He is credited by the fourth century BCE geographer Agathemenus with being the first 'to draw the inhabited world on a tablet',[5] in other words the first map.

Anaximenes, (c.585 - 528 BCE) and said to be a student of Anaximander, believed that air could change into different forms. By condensation and purification air could be made to create the world and everything in it. When air was purified or rarefied it became the element fire and when condensed it changed into wind, cloud, water, \earth or

---

[5] Geographi Graeces Minores, Muller, 1855.

stone. Air therefore was divine. Anaximenes also believed that the earth was flat and floated on air. The planets, to him, were fiery leaves.

The water clock was called a *clepsydra*, literal meaning '*a water thief*', in ancient Greek. It worked by allowing water to trickle into a cistern. In this water was a float that operated a pointer, and it was the pointer which told the time.

Neither the early water clocks nor the sundials were very accurate. But to the ancients it was not so important to be as very exact with time as in today's hectic world, where every second counts.

THE NAMING OF THE DAYS

Now to how the days were actually named. This is quite complex. They were originally named after the classical planets: Moon, Mars, Mercury, Jupiter, Venus, Saturn, and the Sun. This is strange because of course, modern names of the day's bear little relation to these original planets. But let us look more closely.

To take the first one from this list of celestial spheres, the Moon. Monday the first day after the weekend, derives its name from the Latin *Lunae dies* or moon day.

Now to take the next one on the list, Mars. Tuesday's day gets its name from the Teutonic god Tiw, god of war and the sky. This corresponds with the Roman god, Mars. Thus Tuesday has a link with Mars.

Now to take the planet Mercury, how does this link with Wednesday? Well Wednesday comes from the Anglo-Saxon god of war Woden. This corresponds with the Roman god Mercury. In France the day is called by the more correct Mercredi, still alluding to its planetary origins.

Right, now to take the planet Jupiter and Thursday. Thursday has its name from the Germanic god of thunder Thor. It was Thor's day, thus Thursday. Thor corresponds to the Roman god Jupiter who also threw thunderbolts.

Now the planet Venus. Here we have the Germanic goddess of love Frigg. Friday takes its name from this ancient goddess. Frigg concurs with the Roman love goddess Venus. Originally the day was the Latin *Veneris dies*, the day of Venus. In France it is still called Vendredi, keeping to its primary source.

The next planet, Saturn is nearer in translation to the day Saturday. The Roman for Saturday is *Saturni dies*, the day of Saturn. This seems to be the only day which does not use a Norse equivalent, although there is a Northern god called Sataere which was one of the many names of the god Loki.

The Sun is associated with the day of Sunday. It comes from the Latin, *dies Solis*, the day of the Sun. Although this was originally a pagan solar symbol, it has gradually been taken to become a description of the Christian god. In the bible, God is described as: *"Sun of righteousness"*,[6] or as *"sun and shield"*.[7] This is very much in keeping with the fact that Sunday is the Christian Sabbath, a holy day, devoted to the praise of God. In France this is clearer; their name for the day is Dimanche, coming from the Latin *'dies dominicus'* which translates as *"day of the Lord"*. The Germanic pagan name has been given Christian symbolism.

That's how the days got their modern titles which are used today, from ancient Roman and Saxon gods (who come from the same Germanic roots as the Norse gods). They were all originally named directly or indirectly after their representative planets. But that brings us to another question. Why were they in that order? For the answer we have to look at astronomy.

In the planetary week the sequence of days corresponded to the order of the planets according to their distance from the earth. Saturn was the furthest away from the Earth the Moon the nearest. The actual order of the planets in relation to the earth is as follows, taking the outer planets first: Saturn, Jupiter, Mars, Sun, Venus, Mercury, and the Moon. Now it gets very complex.

Each hour of the twenty four hour day was allotted to a planet. The first hour was allotted to the planet furthest from the earth, Saturn. The sequence of planets was repeated with each hour attributed to the next hour until after seven hours and all the list of planets exhausted, you come to the eighth hour. This was given to the first planet of the list again, Saturn. This cycle was repeated for every hour of the day. So the first hour of Saturday would be Saturn's as would the eighth, the fifteenth and the twenty second. The twenty-third hour would go to the next planet, Jupiter, and the twenty-fourth to Mars. Now we are left with the first hour of the next day. This would be the sun and the next day therefore started at the hour of the sun and was Sunday.

Thus you had the sequence of the week, each day marked by the planetary cycle. The week was now ruled by the planets. This planetary week became common in the

---

6 Malachi 4:2.
7 Psalm 84:11.

West under the Emperor Augustus. But it was actually made into law by the Emperor Constantine, who sanctified the astrological week in 321 CE when he ordered that *"all judges and urban merchants abstain from working on the venerable day of the sun"*.[8]

---

[8] Justinian Codex 3.2.3.

PART 2
ANGLO-SAXON, NORSE &
CHRISTIAN WORLDVIEWS

THE ANGLO-SAXON WORLD
IN THE AGE OF THE VIKINGS

In this period most tradition was oral, and not much was written down. This leaves us with a difficulty in trying to picture life all those centuries ago. For life must have been different in England to that of the Viking in Scandinavia. Undoubtedly the basis of the religion was the same. The gods were the same, although the names were slightly different, Woden for Odin for example. But Germanic and Norse gods were called upon in England.

Unfortunately there are not many surviving epics from England during this period. Most information comes from the *Eddas* from Iceland. But England does have its saga. This was the epic, *Beowulf*. Although it is English the poem itself describes a Germanic hero. Jan de Vries in his *Heroic Song and Heroic Legend* says that: *"there is no stranger poem in the whole of Germanic heroic poetry."*[9]

It is a mixing of historical characters with mythological legend. Some of the people mentioned are found in historical sources. There is the English King Offa, a descendant of the Old English kings of Mercia. There are Hengest and Finn, historical characters in Kent. The King of the Geats, Hygelac, is found in Frankish historical sources. The Danish King Hrothgar (version of the modern name of Roger) was also an actual ruler. The poem contains reports of the fights with the Swedes which are one of the principle sources of our knowledge of the history of Sweden in the early Middle Ages. But it is not known if the hero of the epic *Beowulf* was an actual historical figure.

The date of *Beowulf* is considered to be between the 8th and the early 11th centuries. The events described in the poem take place between the late 5th century, after the Anglo-Saxons had begun migration and settlement in England, and the beginning of the 7th century, a time when

---

[9] Heroic Song and Heroic Legend, de Vries, 1963:55.

the Saxons were either newly arrived or in close contact with their fellow Germanic kinsmen in Scandinavia and Northern Germany. It has been suggested that *Beowulf* was first composed in the 7th century at Rendlesham in East Anglia, as Sutton Hoo also shows close connections with Scandinavia, and also that the East Anglian royal dynasty, the Wuffings, were descendants of the Geatish Wulfings. Others have associated this poem with the court of King Alfred, or with the court of King Canute.

The story itself is about the life of a warrior prince called Beowulf. At the court of the Danish King Hrothgar, there was a monster called Grendel. This monster creates absolute havoc. At night he appears in the king's hall and abducts thirty men. This happens night after night for twelve long years. The men are slaughtered in a horrific manner and there was great sorrow in the court.

The poem *Beowulf* is a mixture of Pagan and Christian thought. That is evident in the description of the monster Grendel, here from the Hall translation:

> *"That grim spirit was called Grendel, the renowned traverser of the marches, who held the moors, the fens, and fastness; unblessed creature, he dwelt for a while in the lair of monsters, after the Creator had condemned them. On Cain's kindred the everlasting Lord avenge the murder, for that he had slain Abel; he had no joy of that feud, but the Creator drove him far from mankind for that misdeed. Thence all evil broods were born, ogres and elves and evil spirits - the giants also, who long time fought with God, for which he gave them their reward."*[10]

In this extract, when evil spirits are mentioned this comes from the word *Orcneas*. This is from the Latin root *orc*, from *orcus* meaning 'the underworld' or Hades and *neas* meaning 'corpses'. This could be taken as a reference to necromancy, the art of revealing future events by communicating with the dead. This was common in Germany and in England where it was revived by the invading Vikings. The newly buried dead could be made to call up the spirits that inhabited them. To the Christians this

---

[10] Beowulf and the Finnesburg Fragment, Hall, 1950.

would have made them evil spirits. They would not necessary have been evil to the pagans. It is a good example of the Christianization of pagan legend.

Beowulf offers to slay Grendel, and free the court from fear. He stays the night at the king's hall. Sure enough the monster Grendel appears and tries to drag Beowulf from the building. But Beowulf fights back, and the huge monster's arm is torn off. Grendel flees, leaving a trail of blood leading to a lake. Here at the water he was killed, as the poem rather gruesomely describes it:

> *"Then the water was boiling with blood, the frightful surge of the waves welled up, all mingled with hot gore - with sword-blood; death doomed creature had hidden himself there, and then, deprived of joys, he gave up his life - his heathen soul in the fen-refuge; there hell received him!"*[11]

Now our hero is attacked by Grendel's mother who wants to avenge her son's death. Beowulf arms himself to attack the monster. Here in the epic is a wonderful description of armour of the period, you can really picture it:

> *"Beowulf arrayed himself with princely armour; no whit did he feel anxious for his life. His war-corselet, woven by hand, ample and deftly worked, was to make trial of the mere. It had power to shield his body, so that for him the battle-grasp, the fury's vengeful grip, might do no damage to his breast, his life: The shining helmet screened his head, which was to stir up the watery depths, to tempt the churning waves. It was adorned with gold, encircled with lordly bands, as in past days the weapon-smith had wrought it, - formed it wondrously, and set it round with boar-images, so that after that no sword or battle-knife could ever cut through it. That, too, was not the least of mighty aids, which Hrothgar's spokesman lent him in his need. Hrunting was the name of that hilted sword, which was one among the foremost of ancient heirlooms. The blade was iron, patterned by twigs of venom, hardened with blood of battle. Never had it failed any man in time of war, of those who grasped it with their hands, who dared enter upon perilous adventures, the*

---

[11] Ibid.

meeting place of foes: - not the first time was that, that it had bold work to do."[12]

Thus did Beowulf arm himself to confront the ogress in her watery home, a lake. He is dragged down into an underground cave. Here he battles for his life. In this cave is an ancient sword. Beowulf seizes it. Now he can confront the monster and kill her. Inspecting the underground vault he finds the body of Grendel. Beowulf cuts of the brute's head to take back as a trophy. But all this fighting and bloodletting had stained the water blood red. Hrothgar's men return home convinced that Beowulf is dead. Beowulf's own followers however, have more faith in their leader and wait. Their patience is rewarded and they and Beowulf return to the hall of King Hrothgar in triumph.

After the death of the king of the Geats, Beowulf becomes king and reigns for fifty years. The next part of the saga concerns Beowulf and his fight with a fire breathing dragon. This dragon guards a hoard, a wealth of treasure which was the rich spoils of a generation of brave warriors. All this fortune was hidden in a cave where it is guarded by the dragon for three hundred years. But an outlaw finds the treasure and steals a precious goblet. The dragon awakes and realises that his precious hoard has been ransacked and an object removed. The dragon takes revenge and the whole country trembles in fear. The fire breathing dragon creates havoc with his flames:

> *"The fiend began to vomit forth flames, to born noble dwelling; the gleam of fire blazed forth, a terror to the sons of men; the hateful creature flying in the air would leave there no thing with life. The serpent's warfare was widely visible, the vengeance of the devastation far and near - how the warlike enemy hated and humbled the Geat people."*[13]

The Geats (Old English *Geatas*) were a North Germanic tribe inhabiting what is now Götaland (*'land of the Geats'*) in modern Sweden.

---

[12] Ibid.
[13] Ibid

Figure 1 - Beowulf

The population lived in fear and asked Beowulf to don armour again and protect them. Beowulf was now an old man, but in answer to the people's pleas he had made for him a fireproof shield of iron. This he used and went to out to face and fight the dragon in his lair single handed.

> *"Beowulf spoke: 'I ventured on many battles in my younger days; once more will I, the aged guardian of the people, seek combat and get renown, it the evil ravager will meet me outside this earthy vault.' Then he addressed all of the men, brave under their helmets, his close companions, for the last time. 'I would not bear a sword or weapon against the serpent, if I knew how else I might come to grips with monster in such manner as to fulfil my boast, as I did aforetime against Grendel. But there I look for hot destructive fire, for blast and venom; therefore I have upon me shield and corselet. I will not flee the space of a foot from the guardian of the mound: but at the rampart it shall be to us two as Fate, the lord of every man, decides. I am eager in spirit, so that I forbear from boasting against the winged fighter.*
>
> *Watch on the barrow, ye warriors in your armour, defended by coats of mail, which of us two can endure wounds best, after the desperate onslaught. That is not your affair, nor a possibility for any man, save for me alone, to put forth his power against the monster, and so heroic deeds. By my valour I will win gold; or war, the dread destroyer of life, shall carry off your lord!'"*[14]

Thus Beowulf prepared to fight the fire breathing dragon. A desperate struggle ensues. The dragon belches fire and more flame. Beowulf is in trouble. But help is at hand. Wiglaf, a Scylfing prince, joins in the fray, assisting his master in his hour of need. The dragon turns and attacks Wiglaf. Beowulf seizes his chance and drives his sword into the monsters head, but the sword snaps. Beowulf now draws his knife and thrusts it into the dragon's middle. The dragon is dead at last. But Beowulf is mortally wounded in the battle. During the fight the dragon had bitten Beowulf in the neck, this wound was bloody, the blood seeping out in torrents. Beowulf was dying.

---

[14] Ibid

Figure 2 - Dragon Guardian

The cave was now open and Wiglaf entered it. He was amazed by what he saw. Vast amounts of treasure including precious gold, costly ornaments, goblets and dishes. He carried the treasure to Beowulf so that he could see it before he died. Our hero is overcome:

> *"I utter in words my thanks to the Ruler of all, the King of Glory, the everlasting Lord, for the treasures which I here gaze upon, in that I have been allowed to win such things for my people before my day of death! Now that I have given my old life in barter for the hoard of treasure, do ye henceforth supply the people's needs -I may stay here no longer.*
>
> *Bid the war-veterans raise a splendid barrow after the funeral fire, on a projection by the sea, which shall tower high on Hronesness as a memorial for my people, so that seafarers who urge their tall ships from afar over the spray of ocean shall thereafter call it Beowulf's barrow."*[15]

Thus Beowulf dies. The people of Geat then prepare for his funeral. This funeral is evocatively described in the poem, one of the most rousing and moving descriptions of a Norse cremation:

> *"The people of the Geats then made ready for him on the ground a firm-built funeral pyre, hung round with helmets, battle-shields, bright corselets, as he had begged them to do. Then mighty men, lamenting, laid in its midst the famous prince, their beloved lord. The warriors then began to kindle on the mount the greatest of funeral pyres; the dark wood-smoke towered above the blazing mass; the roaring flame mingled with the noise of weeping - the raging of the winds had ceased - till it had crumbled up the body, hot to its core,. Depressed in soul they uttered forth their misery, and mourned their lord's death. Moreover, the Geatish woman with hair bound up, sang in memory of Beowulf a doleful dirge and said repeatedly that she greatly feared evil days for herself, much carnage, the terror of the foe, humiliation and captivity. Heaven swallowed up the smoke."*[16]

---

[15] Ibid.
[16] Ibid.

The rest of Beowulf's instructions were carried out. A high and broad barrow was built on a cliff which would act a as beacon. This was placed over his remains. In this beacon was placed gold, the wealth of nobles, left in the ground, as a memorial to a hero. Twelve chieftains rode round the barrow, lamenting their king in a dirge. He was praised for his bravery. It was a fitting monument to a courageous, bold, and brave warrior king.

Beowulf is the oldest epic in English. It is difficult to trace its roots. There is a story about the monster Grendel in the Old Norse saga of Grettir, an Icelandic saga ascribed to Grettir Asmundarson who died in c. 1031 CE. There is also an old Irish fairy tale in which a monsters arm is hacked off by the hero, similar to the fate of Grendel's arm in Beowulf. Jan de Vries in *Heroic Song and Heroic Legend* ascribes to the theory that both *Beowulf* and the Icelandic saga go back to a Danish or Swedish poem.

The image of the dragon guarding treasure is a familiar one in mythology. In the classical literature of Greece the dragon Ladon guarded the golden apples in the garden of Hesperides. He was slain by Hercules as the eleventh of his *'twelve labours'* and the apples taken to Eurystheus, king of Mycenae, who imposed these twelve dangerous labours on Hercules.

Again in Greek mythology there is the story of Cadmus, who introduced the alphabet into Greece. Part of the story involved the slaying of a dragon that guarded the fountain of Dirce in Boeotia, the ancient name for a district in central Greece. Cadmus planted the teeth of the monster which grew into a number of armed men. Cadmus consulted the goddess Athena, who advised him to throw a precious stone among the soldiers. This he did. The soldiers all fought among themselves, killing each other in the process for possession of the gemstone. There were five survivors and these men helped build the city of Cadmea, which became Thebes. The phrase *'to sow dragon's teeth'* became a way of saying, to stir up war or strife, or to do something to end war but which in turn brings about hostility and war.

The dragon was a popular symbol in Pagan times. The Norse painted dragons on their shields and carved dragons head on the prows of their longships. To the Romans the dragon was the insignia of the cohort, the tenth part of a Roman legion. A cohort consisted of six centuries or bodies of soldiers. Saxon kings of England had dragons on their standards.

The dragon was associated with paganism. When the country was converted to Christianity the dragon became a symbol of sin in general and paganism in particular. In fact Satan was called *'the great dragon'*. This is how the dragon is symbolised in art. The metaphor continued with many saints being depicted as dragon killers. Perhaps the most famous of these are St Michael and St George.

These were superstitious days. Some of the old Anglo-Saxon pagan imagery survived in ancient charms. These were incantations to remedy illness and such things as the barrenness of land. Here is a charm that quite clearly evokes a pagan goddess and earth worship:

> *"Erce, Erce, Erce, Mother of Earth...*
> *Hail to thee, Earth, mother of men!*
> *Be fruitful in God's embrace,*
> *Filled with food for the use of men."*[17]

> *"Then take every kind of meal and have a loaf baked no bigger than the palm of your hand, having kneaded it with milk and holy water, and lay it under the first turned furrow."*[18]

This charm contains an appeal to the sun. Both it and the one about the earth are from the charm for increasing the fertility of the earth. This charm was called *Aecerbot*, the *'Remedy for Cultivated Land'*. Of course the fertility of the crops was a common pagan theme. The Gods were often evoked in an attempt to increase the harvest. But here is the charm:

> *"Turn to the east and bowing humbly nine times say then these words:*
> *Eastwards I stand, for favours I pray*
> *I pray the great Lord, I pray the mighty Prince*
> *I pray the holy Warden of the heavenly kingdom*
> *To earth I pray and to up-heaven...*

---

[17] Cotton MS Caligula A.vii.
[18] Cotton MS Caligula A.vii.

Then turn three times sunwise and stretch yourself along the ground full length and say the litany there...."[19]

This charm is a wonderful example of the fusion of Pagan and Christian beliefs. There is a charm for a swarm of Bees that again clearly shows the importance of the earth, another pagan doctrine:

Concerning a swarm of bees. Take earth in your right hand; cast it under right foot and say:
"I have it underfoot; I have found it.
Behold! Earth avails against all kinds of creatures,
it avails against malice and evil jealousy
and against the mighty tongue of man."
When they swarm, scatter earth over them and say:
"Alight, victorious women, alight on the earth!
Never turn wild and fly to the woods!
Be just as mindful of my benefit
as is every man of his food and his fatherland!"[20]

Here is another interesting charm which describes a ritual using a dung beetle and earth to cure a stomach ache:

Against stomach-ache and pain in the abdomen. When you see a dung-beetle throw up earth, catch it between your hands together with the heap. Wave it vigorously with your hands and say three times:
Remedium facio ad ventris dolorem
Then throw away the beetle over your back and take care that you do not look after it.
When a man's stomach or abdomen pains him, catch the belly between your hands.
He will soon be better.
For twelve months you may do so after catching the beetle.[21]

That last charm appears to contain instructions for what is now called hands on healing, spiritual healing, or faith healing. Using your hands to heal has a long history.

There is also *Bald's Leechbook*. This was a medical book compiled in the late ninth or early tenth century in

---

[19] Cotton MS Caligula A.vii.
[20] Cambridge MS 41, C11th CE.
[21] MS Cotton Julius C2.

Winchester, possibly under the influence of Alfred the Great's educational reforms. Interestingly in *Bald's Leechbook* is the only plastic surgery mentioned in Anglo-Saxon records. The recipe in particular prescribes surgery for a hare lip. Bald was the owner, of whom unfortunately not much is known. Here are some extracts:

> *"If a man be over-virile, boil water agrimony in welsh ale; he is to drink it at night, fasting. If a man be insufficiently virile, boil the same herb in milk; then you will excite it. Again: boil in ewe's milk: water agrimony, alexanders, the herb called Fornet's palm. so it will be as he most desires.*
>
> *Against a woman's chatter: eat a radish at night, while fasting; that day the chatter cannot harm you.*
>
> *Make thus a salve against the race of elves, goblins and those women with whom the Devil copulates; take the female hop-plant, wormwood, betony, lupin, vervain, henbane, dittander, viper's bugloss, bilberry plants, cropleek, garlic, madder grains, corn cockle, fennel. Put those plants in a vat; place under an altar; sing nine masses over it; boil it in butter and in sheep's grease; add much holy salt; strain through a cloth; throw the herbs into running water; If any evil temptation come to a man, or elf or goblin, anoint his face with this salve; And put it on his eyes and there his body is sore, and cense him and frequently sign him with the cross; his condition will soon be better."[22]*

Here follows an extract from what was known as the *Nine Herbs Charm.*[23] This clearly mentions Woden, the Anglo-Saxon version of the Norse god Odin. There are also references to serpents, symbolising paganism and to Christ himself. There is also many references to the number nine. Nine was a spiritual number to those of the Old Religion. There were nine worlds according to the Norse beliefs. The poem also refers to seven worlds. This is common in Greek classical literature; there were seven heavens or planets to the ancients. It is a fascinating example of the blending of the two religions of the time:

> *"A snake came crawling, it bit a man.*

---

[22] MS Royal 12.D, xvii
[23] Sections 79-83, Harley MS 585

Then Woden took nine glory-twigs,
Smote the serpent so that it flew into nine parts.
There Apple brought this to pass against poison,
That she nevermore would enter her house.

Thyme and Fennel, a pair great in power,
The Wise Lord, holy in heaven,
Wrought these herbs while He hung on the cross;
He placed and put them in the seven worlds

To aid all, poor and rich.
It stands against pain, resists the venom,
It has power against three and against thirty,
Against witchcraft of vile creatures.

Now these nine herbs avail against nine evil spirits,
Against nine poisons and against nine infectious
diseases...
If any poison comes flying from the east or any comes
from the north,
Or any from the west upon the people.

Christ stood over disease of every kind.
I alone know of running water, and the nine serpents
heed it;
May all pastures now spring up with herbs,
The sea, all salt water, be destroyed,
When I blow this poison from thee."

Clearly the old pagan ways echoed in the medical knowledge of the era. These old charms offer fascinating glimpses into the past lifestyles of the Anglo-Saxons.

The Anglo-Saxon world was very different to the one of today. This difference is shown most in the Anglo-Saxon legal code. The laws of these ancient people make fascinating reading. They reveal a totally distinct attitude to the law, which may seem strange to modern eyes.

Lawsuits were conducted before assemblies, called folk-moots, later as the legal system evolved, hundred courts, borough courts and shire courts. The defendant would make an oath. Now oath-helpers would be called upon to testify to his innocence. If the person could not muster enough supporters to plead for his innocence or was found guilty, he was given a choice. He could either pay a fine or he could elect to trial by ordeal.

The ordeals varied, for churchmen it was for them to eat plenty of consecrated bread or cheese. Those who choked were guilty. For the laymen it was a lot harder. They were bound and thrown into a pool of water. If the poor individual sank, he was guilty, if he floated he was innocent. This was called the cold water ordeal. It was believed that water had magical and purifying properties. Therefore being held underwater, God would decide their guilt.

During the Middle Ages this form of torture was commonly used for suspected witches. The whole ceremony was carried out under the direction of a priest. The minister would intone:

> "I conjure you, O man! In the name of the Father, of the Son, and of the Holy Ghost; by the Christian religion which you profess; by Jesus, the only begotten son of God; by the Holy Trinity; by the Holy Gospels, and by all the holy relics of the Church, that you presume not to draw near to the altar, or to receive the communion, if you are guilty of the crime whereof you are accused; or, if you have consented to it; or, know by whom it was committed."[24]

Now the priest prayed. The person was stripped naked, bound hand and foot. A rope was tied round his waist and knotted at about half a yard from the body (45cm). He was then thrown into the water till the knot disappeared under the water.

In the Anglo-Saxon days the ritual was slightly different. In the Laws of Aethelstan, (ruled 924-936 CE) the distance of the rope on which the poor individual had to sink was one and half ells. An ell was 45 inches (114cm). So the distance was longer. The way the victim was tied was different as well. The thumb of his right hand was tied to the big toe of his left foot, and the left hand thumb to his opposite toe on his right foot.

Drowning as a form of execution was quite common in many civilisations. In ancient Rome, this was the sentence for the crimes of bigamy and patricide, the killing of one's

---

[24] History of Torture Throughout the Ages, Scott, 1995:231.

father. In France during the reign of Charles IV (1380-1392 CE), known as Charles the Mad, or the Well-Beloved, the crime of sedition was punished by drowning.

Another ordeal for the laymen was to carry a piece of molten iron for an agreed distance. That sounds very painful. This piece of iron weighed anything between two and three pounds. It was heated until it was red hot, and this smouldering lump of iron was carried in the bare hands of the accused. Sometimes the victim would be forced to walk with naked feet and blindfolded over nine red-hot ploughshares laid on the ground at unequal distances. Very painful!

In the laws of Aethelstan, strict codes of conduct were enforced regarding this ordeal of iron:

> *"If anyone pledges (to undergo) the ordeal, he is then to come three days before to the priest whose duty it is to consecrate it, and live off bread and water and salt and vegetables until he shall go to it, and be present at mass on each of those three days, and make his offering and go to communion on the day on which he shall go to the ordeal, and swear then the oath that he is guiltless of that charge according to the common law, before he goes to the ordeal."*[25]

It appears to have been very much a religious experience. The mother of Edward the Confessor (c.1003-66 CE), Queen Emma was accused of adultery with Alwyn, Bishop of Winchester. It must have been a big scandal. But the queen was able to prove her innocence by electing to go through this ordeal. She received no injury and was thus innocent of all charges against her.

This form of torture was common in many other cultures. The ancient Greek tragedian, Sophocles (c.496-406 BCE) mentions it. Fire was used to prove the innocence of the Holy Roman Empress Richarda (844-900 CE), the wife of Charles the Fat. She was accused of adultery with Bishop Luitward. The Empress' champion walked through the flames of a blazing fire, thus proving her innocence.

---

[25] Of Him Who Gives Wed For An Ordeal, Aethelstans Laws, in Thorpe 2004:90.

It is strange that a great many people seemed to be able to prove their innocence by going through this horrible and painful ordeal without receiving any burns. An option was for the metal to be heated till it was white hot rather than red hot; it could now be touched with safety. But whether there was any collusion between those of a high rank and the officiating priest is unknown.

There was also the trial by ordeal of boiling water. Now a naked hand was placed in boiling water to lift a heavy ball. The hand was now bound by the priest and left for three days. It was now uncovered, if unblemished, the accused was innocent. There do appear to be ways round this form of torture if you know them. It was thought that you would be unscathed if you first rubbed the skin with spirit of vitriol and alum mixed with the juice of onions.

There is wonderful description of the trial by ordeal, hot iron and water, in the Laws of Aethelstan. Here it is:

"And concerning the ordeal we enjoin by the command of God., and of the archbishop, and of all the bishops; that no man come within the church after the fire is borne in with which the ordeal shall be heated, except the mass-priest, and him who shall go thereto. Let there be measured nine feet from the stake to the mark, by the man's feet who goes thereto. But if it be water, let it be heated till it low to boiling. And be the kettle of iron or of brass or of lead or of clay. And if it be a single accusation, let the man dive after the stone up to the wrist; and if it be threefold, up to the elbow.

And when the ordeal is ready, then let two men, go in of either side; be they agreed that it is so hot as we before have said. And let go in an equal number of men of either side and stand on both sides of the ordeal, along the church; and let these all be fasting on that night, and abstinent from their wives on that night; and let the mass-priest sprinkle holy-water over them all, and let each of them taste of the holy water, and give them all the book and the image of Christ's rood to kiss. And let no man mend the fire any longer when the hallowing is begun; but let the iron lie upon the hot embers till the last collect; after that, let it be laid upon the 'stepela' (pile of wood), and let there be no other speaking within, except that they earnestly pray to Almighty God that He make manifest what is soothest.

And let him go thereto; an let his hand be enveloped, and be it postponed till after the third day, whether it be foul or clean within the envelope. And he who shall break this law, be the ordeal with respect to him void, and let him pay to the king one hundred and twenty shillings as 'wite' (fine)."[26]

The punishments were certainly harsh in the days of the Anglo-Saxons.

When the Vikings overran England they left their mark in the names of different parts of the countryside. In many parts of the country, especially the eastern sector you can find words such as: Beck, meaning *'stream'*; Brigg, meaning *'bridge'*; Carr, meaning *'marsh'*; Dale, *'share of land'*; Garth, *'enclosure'*; Gate, *'way'*, *'road'* or *'street'*; Kirk, *'church'*; Lathe, *'barn'* and Roe and Wroe, meaning *'corner of land'*, *'secluded spot'*. All these words are of a Scandinavian origin.

The invaders were often referred to as the Danes although they were also from Norway and Frisia. Frisia extended from the north-western Netherlands across north-western Germany to the border of Denmark. This is reflected in many names of places in eastern England. In Lincolnshire and the West Riding of Yorkshire there are sites called Normanby, meaning *'village of the Norwegians'*. There is also Normanton in Devon, Lincolnshire, Leicestershire, Rutland, and the West Riding of Yorkshire, which has a similar origin. Both Firsby in Lincolnshire and Frisby in Leicestershire mean *'village of the Frisians'*. Danby in the North Riding of Yorkshire, Denaby in the West Riding of Yorkshire, and Denby in Derbyshire, have the meaning *'village of the Danes'*. But before we think that the whole country was covered in Norse settlements, there in south Derbyshire there is Ingleby, the *'village of the English'*, obviously an important place to the native inhabitants. It does seem strange, though for a village to be known as the village of the English in England. There must have been an awful lot of Norse in the area. It shows how the invasion of the Northmen must have really affected the country.

---

[26] Doom Concerning Hot Iron and Water, Aethelstans Laws, in Thorpe, 2004: 96.

Evidence of the old pagan worship can be found in place names. There are two Old English definitions of 'heathen shrine', 'haerg' or 'hearg' and 'weoh' or 'wih', 'wig'. The first is found in the site of Harrowden in Bedfordshire and Northamptonshire, this means the 'hill with a pagan shrine' and in Harrow on the Hill in Middlesex. The latter term for 'shrine' is found in Wye in Kent and Wyham in Lincolnshire. It is also found as a component of a name such as Weedon in Buckinghamshire, and Weedon Bec and Weedon Lois in Northamptonshire, 'shrine on a hill'. The same applies to Weeford in Staffordshire, shrine at a ford. Wheely in Farnham and Whiligh in Ticehurst, both in Surrey, means 'shrine at sacred glade'. There are many other examples of pagan shrines hidden in the names of places in the countryside.

The old Saxon pagan gods are also found in place names. These are mainly the gods Tiw, Woden, Thunor or Thor, and Frigg. As already seen they are found in the day names of, Tuesday, Wednesday, Thursday, and Friday, respectively.

Tiw, origin of Tuesday, was a war god. His name is reflected in Tysmere in Worcestershire, the name being 'Tiw's pool'. There is also Tysoe, in Warwickshire, the name meaning 'Tiw's hill spur'. This is particularly interesting as this is situated above the Vale of the Red Horse. This is a horse cut out of the hill side. It could be representing the god Tiw. But here this animal could also portray the earlier Celtic goddess Epona, often depicted with a horse.

Now we have Woden as the origin of Wednesday. Echoes of his name are found in many places in the Midlands and the South. There was a shrine dedicated to him at Wednesbury, meaning 'Woden's fortress', in Staffordshire. Near Wednesbury is Wednesfield, 'Woden's field', both of these are situated above the River Thame. They are only five miles apart and this suggests quite a following for the ancient god in that area. There is also Wensley meaning 'Woden's sacred grove' in Derbyshire; and Woodensborough, near Sandwich in Kent, which has the meaning of 'Woden's tumulus'. There are many other places in the country associated with Woden.

Woden also seems to be well represented at Wansdyke, called Woden's dic in the 10th century, an earthwork that runs from Hampshire through Wiltshire to Somerset. Dic is the Old English for *'ditch'*. This a massive earthworks, only perhaps surpassed by the later Offa's Dyke. It follows an earlier Roman road and archaeological excavations confirm that it belongs to the early part of the Dark Ages. We have no idea why such an immense structure was built and dedicated to the great god Odin, which is the Norse name for Woden. There are further conformations of the influence of Odin in the names of places near the earthworks. Here there are Wodnes beorge, meaning *'Woden's barrow'*, this is a Neolithic long barrow now known as Adam's Grave by Alton Priors, and Wones dene, meaning *'Woden's Valley'* now known as Hursley Bottom near West Overton.

Woden had many nicknames, one of which was Grim. The word comes from the Old English *'grima'*, meaning *'mask'* and used for a person who wears a hood masking his face. It is a reference to Odin's habit of wandering from the world of the gods to the world of man in disguise. Grim is often associated with earthworks. There is a Grim's Ditch in Berkshire, Hampshire, Oxfordshire, and Wiltshire. Similarly there is a Grim's Dike in Hampshire and the West Riding of Yorkshire. Woden was said to have been the creator of these vast ramparts. Interestingly there are twice as many names derived from Grim as there are for Woden. This suggests that when the country was converted to Christianity, Woden's nickname survived more than the god himself.

Now we have Thunor or Thor, origin of Thursday, and god of thunder. Thunor is commonly found in place names in the counties of Essex and Wessex. In fact in those two areas of the country he appears to be more widespread than the great god Woden. Nearly all the traces of Thunor in place names appears to be in the south of the country, he is absent from the midlands and the north. This suggests that Thunor was a Saxon or Jutish deity. Thunor gave his name to Thunderfield and Thursley both in Surrey, Thunderley and Thurdersley both in Essex, Thundreslea near Southampton, meaning *'sacred glade'* and Thunreslea near Droxford both in Hampshire. There is also Thunoreshloew near Manston in Kent and Thundridge in Hertfordshire. In

Sussex, Surrey, Essex and Hampshire Thunor's name sometimes precedes the word *'leah'*. This is an Old English word meaning *'wood'* or *'woodland clearing'*. This is interesting as the Roman historian Tacitus wrote of the Germanic gods being worshipped in sacred groves, though the Celts also venerated the gods in sacred groves. This may have been a fusion of the two religions, or perhaps the Saxon gods subsumed the earlier Celtic ones, one pagan faith blending into another.

Now to Frigg, the origin of Friday. She was a fertility goddess and one of the three wives of Odin. Frigg is not found in many names in the country. There is Freefolk in Hampshire. This was called Frigefolc in the *Domesday Book* and could be taken to mean *'Frigg's people'*. There is also Froyle and Frobury in Hampshire. These two places could have been named after this goddess. There is a theory that they both come from the Old English *Freohyll*, meaning *'the hill of (the goddess) Frigg'*. There is also Fryup in the North Riding of Yorkshire. This could mean *'the hop or marshy land of Freo or Frigg'*. There is also Friden near Ballidon in Derbyshire. An Anglo-Saxon document dated 963 CE was found giving this place the spelling Frigedene, which could mean the *'valley of the goddess Frigg'*. But unlike the other gods mentioned, the roots of the place names attributed to Frigg cannot be proven, they are only theories. This goddess seems to have disappeared into thin air.

It is unknown why there are pagan places names in some areas of the country and not in others. These pagan names appear to be mostly south, south eastern, and the centre of the country as far as the north Midlands. Perhaps when England was Christianised, some parts were converted more easily than others.

NORSE PAGANISM AND CHRISTIANITY

How were the Norse viewed? There is a wonderful description of them by an Arab called Al-Tartushi in the *Travel Book of Ibrahim ibn Jakub* in 975 CE. He describes the town of Slesvig and its inhabitants. Here it is:

> *"Slesvig is a large town at the farthest end of the world ocean. Within it there are wells of fresh water. Its inhabitants worship Sirius, apart from a few who are Christians and have a church there. They hold a festival where they assemble to honour their god and eat and drink. Anyone who slaughters an animal by way of sacrifice has a palisade (or pole) outside his house door and hangs the sacrificed animal there, whether it be ox or ram, he-goat or boar, so that people may know that he makes sacrifice in honour of his god. The town is poorly off for goods and wealth. The people's chief food is fish, for there is so much of it. If a child is born there it is thrown into the sea to save bringing it up. Moreover he relates that women have the right to declare themselves divorced: they part with their husbands whenever they like. They also have there an artificial make-up for the eyes; when they use it their beauty never fades, but increases in both man and woman. He said too: I have never heard more horrible singers than the Slevigers' - it is like a growl coming out of their throats, like the barking of dogs only much more beastly."*[27]

Al-Tartushi clearly relates that both Christians and Pagans lived and worshipped openly in harmony together. This is further confirmed by archaeology. Both pagan and Christian graves have been found.

The practice of throwing babies into the sea seems similar to the custom of the Spartans who left weak babies to die to the elements. This would have been seen to strengthen the tribe. Although I find the practice totally

---

[27] A History of the Vikings, Jones, 1984:177.

abhorrent, those were violent days and it was a society based on the strong warrior.

Women appeared to be free to change their partners as often as they wished, a right only recently available to modern women. They cared about how they looked, cosmetics being used by both sexes. In another eye witness account by John of Wallingford there is conformation of their fastidious appearance. He says that the Danes in England combed their hair, took a bath on Saturdays, and changed their clothes when grubby. This made them very attractive to English ladies. It is a totally different picture to the normal one of dirty, raiding pirates.

Evidence of early Christian colonisation of Iceland is by Helgi the Lean, who seemed to want the best of both worlds. He called his estate Kristnes meaning Christ's Headland. But when he was in danger he always evoked the old Norse Thor, just to be on the safe side. Another early settler was Aud the Deepminded. This widow erected crosses on her land which is still called Krossholar, meaning *'Cross Mounds'*. Her nephew, Ketill was also a practising Christian. He however was nicknamed *'the Fool'*, by his pagan neighbours, so perhaps the early Christians of Iceland were tolerated more than understood.

Certainly Iceland was pagan till 1000 CE. This suited the inhabitants. They were violent days. The paganism of the Icelanders had no dogma; it made few ethical or moral demands. For the general population it was easier to follow than Christianity with its subsequent codes of ethics and threats of damnation when these codes were broken. The pagan gods were honoured; sacrifices and prayer were made in their names. But that was the extent of the religious responsibility.

There is not much known about pagan temples. But there are the remains of one at Hofstadir near Myvatn in the north of Iceland. This is a two roomed building facing north-south. In the largest of these rooms there were benches placed for the worshippers. In the smaller room, at the north end of the building it is thought that there were wooden figures representing the gods and goddesses invoked.

There is more information about pagan temples in one of the Icelandic sagas, that of the *Eyrbyggja Saga*. This temple was dedicated to the Norse god Thor, and was built by a settler in Iceland from Norway, Thorolfr. There is a wonderful description of one of the rooms. In the centre of this room, standing on the floor was a pedestal on which there was a great arm ring. This arm ring was specially made and constructed without a join. It weighed twenty ounces, quite a weigh for a piece of religious jewellery. It was on this ring that all oaths had to be sworn, so it was obviously a sacred piece. At public gatherings the priest would wear this holy ring on his arm. Here is the actual description in the saga vividly told. As there is so little known about pagan temples of this period I will quote the full extract:

> "He had a temple built, and it was a mighty building. There was a doorway in the side wall. Nearer to the one end, and inside stood the main pillars (ondvegissulur) in which nails were set, called 'divine nails' (reginnaglar). Within there was a great sanctuary. Further in there was an apartment of the same form as the chancel in churches nowadays, and there was a pedestal in the middle of the floor there like an altar, and upon it lay an armring without a joint, weighing twenty ounces, and all oaths must be sworn upon it. The temple-priest (hofgodi) must wear this ring on his arm at all public gatherings. The sacrificial bowl (hlautbolli) must stand on the pedestal, and there was a sacrificial twig in it, like an aspergillum (stokkull) and with it the blood, which was called 'hlaut', should be sprinkled from the bowl. This was blood of the kind shed when beasts were slaughtered as a sacrifice to the gods. The idols were arranged in this apartment around the pillar."[28]

There is also information on rituals in this saga. A bowl was placed on the pedestal in the hallowed room of the temple. Animals were now sacrificed, their blood collected in the bowl. A wooden twig was dipped in the blood which was sprinkled over the congregation. This holy blood was called 'blaut'. Statues of the gods stood around the pedestal, transforming it into an altar.

---

[28] Myth and Religion of the North, Turville-Petre, 1975:241.

Figure 3 - Temple

Animals were sacrificed. These were usually cattle, horses and domestic beasts. There were fires burned in the middle of the floor and the meat of the poor unfortunate creatures boiled in cauldrons suspended over the fire and eaten. The horse's liver was considered to be particularly sacred, this too was devoured. A sacrificial cup was passed over the flames. This cup and food was consecrated (*signa*), by the chieftain. There was now ceremonial beer drinking, and I think a good time was had by all. First, was the toast to Odin, for victory and the success (*rikis*) of the king. Then toasts were drunk for a fruitful harvest and for peace (*til ars ok fridar*). Now there were toasts for fallen comrades who lay buried in *howes*, which were holes in the ground.

The blood sprinkled everywhere and the toasts were said to be symbolic. The men were now joined to the gods of war and fertility. They were also symbolically and religiously connected to their dead ancestors. Blood was considered divine to the Norsemen. They foretold the future from sacrificial blood.

There were thirty six or thirty nine chief temples in Iceland. These were administered by the godar. In 930 CE there were thirty-six godar, but by the time of the reformation of the Constitution in 963 CE this had increased to thirty nine. The godi were responsible for the upkeep of the temple and for the sacrifice. Temple dues, called *haftollar*, were paid to the hofgodi ('*temple-priest*'). Temples were both political and religious centres.

The root of the word godi is fascinating. It derives from '*god*', and originally meant '*the divine*'. The godi was initially solely a religious function. This later changed and position became more of that of a secular chieftain. They became a political leader of each district and had judicial responsibilities presiding over local assemblies. In fact many chiefs held joint office of godi. The joint office of godi and chief was normally hereditary, this high office passed down through the generations.

The gods were also placated with gifts. This is illustrated in the story of *The Cult of Odin* in the *Viga-Glums Saga*. Thorkell the Tall had been expelled from the area of northern Iceland called Thvera. He decided to pray to Freyr to evoke the gods help. He entered the temple of Freyr with an aged ox, to give as a devotion to the god:

> "'Freyr,' said he, 'you who have long been my patron, and accepted many gifts and repaid them well, now I give (gef) you this ox, so that Glum may leave the land of Thvera no less compelled than I leave it now. Let some sign be seen whether you accept or reject it.'"[29]

At this the ox gave a bellow and dropped down dead. Thorkell had his answer; the gods had listened to his plea.

This is a different ritual to the other blood sacrifice. The animal is not actually killed. It is a gift to the gods for them to do with what they wish. It illustrates that the Norse had various forms of ceremonies and sacrifice.

But back to blood sacrifices, the Icelandic chronicler Snorri relates a story about the reign of King Domaldi in Sweden. There was a dreadful famine in the country. The people were hungry. They tried to appease the gods. In the first autumn oxen were sacrificed. But still the crops failed. The second autumn the Swedes sacrificed men. But still the harvest was poor and the people starving. Now the populace decided that the gods needed an even greater sacrifice. They fell upon their king and reddened the altars with his blood. In fact Snorri says that the Swedes reddened the earth with the blood of their lord. Another version of the story says that the king was hanged on a tree. But it is possible that the king was hanged and his blood shed for the protection of the crops. It was considered that these rituals were either dedicated to the war god Odin, or Freya, the goddess of war and death.

This is interesting because in many cultures the kings are considered divine. But when something happens such as losing a war, or the failure of crops, they are considered to have lost their divine right to rule. Snorri in *The Prose Edda* says that the ruling kings of Scandinavia were of divine origin, tracing their decent from the god Odin. The Norse called this divine right of kings 'gaefa' or 'heil'. When this was lost the king could and should be killed.

Human sacrifices were part of the worship of the god Odin. The ancient myths recount how people were either

---

[29] Myth and Religion of the North, Turville-Petre, 1975:252.

hung or stabbed with a spear as an offering to Odin. In fact two of the god's names are *'God of the Hanged'* (*hanga-Tyr*) and *'God of the Spear'* (*galga farmr*).

An example of this is in the story about the champion Starkad in the *Gautreks Saga* reproduced in Turnville-Petre's *Myth and Religion of the North*. I am afraid that it is a long extract, but it clearly shows the Norse attitude to human sacrifice to the gods so I have included it in its entirety:

> *"The famous champion, Starkad, was one of Odin's favourites. Together with his foster-brother, King Vikar of Agdir (South-West Norway), and a number of other champions, he engaged in warlike ventures in coastal districts. The King esteemed none of his champions so highly as Starkad, and they fought together for fifteen years. It happened once that the party lay becalmed off an island and, casting sacrificial chips to find out how to get a favourable wind, they learned that it was Odin's will that one of their number, chosen by lot, should be hanged as a sacrifice to him. When the lots were cast, the name of King Vikar came up, and the champions were dumbfounded. They resolved to meet on the following day. And discuss what steps should be taken.*
>
> *During the night, Starkad was awakened by his old foster-father, who, assuming the name Hrossharsgrani (Horse-hair-bearded), ordered the hero to follow him. They took a boat and rowed to a neighbouring island, where they came to a clearing in the forest. There they found eleven men sitting on chairs, while a twelfth chair stood empty. As Hrossharsgrani sat down in the empty chair, the others greeted him by the name of Odin. Odin told his companions that the time had now come to determine the destiny of Starkad.*
>
> *The first to speak was no other than the god Thor. As the enemy of the giants, Thor had a grudge against Starkad. Starkad descended from giants, for his grandmother had given her favours to a very wise giant (hunviss jotunn) instead of to Thor himself. Thor's first judgement was that Starkad should beget neither son nor daughter, and his race should die with him. But Odin gave it as his judgement that Starkad should have three spans of life, to which Thor replied that he would commit a dastardly act during each one of these three spans. Odin said that Starkad should have*

splendid weapons and treasures a plenty, but Thor said that he would never own land and never be satisfied with that he had. Odin gave Starkad the gift of poetry, saying that he make verse as fast as he could talk, but Thor said that he would never remember a line of his verse. Odin said that Starkad would be prized by the highest and noblest men, but Thor laid down that he would be loathed by all the commonalty.

Then Odin conducted Starkad back to his party, and as he left him, Odin said that he would expect some payment for the great gifts which he had bestowed upon him: Starkad must send King Vikar to him. As he said this, Odin handed the hero a spear, which looked like nothing other than a harmless reed.

When the champions met on the following morning, they resolved to make a token sacrifice of their king. Beside them stood a fir-tree, from which a slender twig drooped, and below it was a stump. The cooks were busy slaughtering a calf, and when the gut was drawn, Starkad tied a noose in it, and hung it on the drooping twig. The king now stepped on to the tree stump; the noose was placed round his neck, and Starkad struck him with a reed, saying: 'Now I give you to Odin'. At that moment, the reed turned into a bitter spear, the stump fell from beneath the king's feet, and the calf's gut became a tough rope. The slender twig was now a stout branch, and it sprang aloft, raising the king to the upper limbs of the tree, where he gave up his life. Starkad had accomplished the first of his dastardly acts."[30]

This is a very interesting tale. It shows vividly how the gods asked for people as a sacrifice and that sacrifice was willingly undertaken. Again a king was considered as a sacrifice. The gods were seen to be able to meet and communicate with man. They actually appeared as men. They could give gifts but expected gifts in return. The life and customs of the Norse are graphically illustrated in this ancient story.

Hanging was a common means of slaughter for sacrifice. Both people and cattle were hung. This was recorded in the

---

[30] Myth and Religion of the North, Turnville-Petre, 1975:44-45.

tenth century by an Arab scientist, Ibn Rustah, who wrote about the Scandinavians in Russia. The priest would decide what was to be sacrificed, a decision totally irrevocable. The victim had now a noose tied round its neck and hung on a pole. The priest intoned: *"this is an offering to god"*.[31]

Another wonderful description of pagan temples is by the German chronicler Adam of Bremen. This was at Uppsala in Sweden. It gives a wonderful feeling of how life was like and is a magnificent portrayal of this religious building, still in use when the author visited it. Here is a summarised account given by Turnville-Petre:

> *"this nation has a most splendid temple called Uppsala, standing not far from the city of Sictona (or Birka). In this temple, totally adorned with gold, the people worship statues of three gods; the most mighty of them, Thor, has his throne in the middle; Wodan and Fricco (Freyr) have their place on either side. Their significance is of this kind: 'Thor', they say, 'rules in the sky, and governs thunder, lightning, the winds, rain, fair weather and produce of the soil.' The second is Wodan, i.e. 'Rage' (furor); he makes wars and gives man bravery in face of enemies. The third is Fricco (Freyr), distributing peace and pleasure among men, whose idol is fashioned with a gigantic 'Priapus', (a fertility god). Wodan they depict armed, as our people depict Mars (Roman god of war). Thor, with his sceptre, seems to resemble Jove (Roman god of lightning, thunder and rain, also known as Jupiter). They also worship gods whom they have made from men and consign to immortality because of great deeds. In the life of St Anskar, so it is recorded they made Eirik (Hericus) a god."*[32]

He further records:

> *"They have priests assigned to all these gods to perform the offerings of the people. If there is danger of pestilence or famine, sacrifice is offered to the idol Thor, if of war to Wodan; if marriage is to be celebrated they offer to Fricco.*
> *It is the practice, every nine years, to hold a communal festival in Ubsola (ancient Uppsala) for all the*

---

[31] Shamanism in Norse Myth and Magic, Tolley, 2009:360.
[32] Myth and Religion of the North, Turnville-Petre, 1975:244.

provinces of Sueonia (ancient Sweden). No exemption from this festival is allowed. The kings and the people, communally and separately, send fits and, most cruel of all, those who have embraced Christianity buy themselves off from these festivities.

The sacrifice is performed thus: nine head of every living male creature are offered, and it is the custom to placate the gods with the blood of these. The bodies are hung in a grove which stands beside the temple. This grove is so holy for the heathens that each of the separate trees is believed to be divine because of the death and gore of the objects sacrifices; there dogs and horses hang with men. One of the Christians (aliquis Christianorum) told me that he had seen seventy-two bodies hanging together. For the rest, the incantations which they are accustomed to sing at this kind of sacrificial rite are manifold and disgraceful, and therefore it is better to be silent about them."[33]

There are three additional notes added to the above comments that are of interest:

"Beside this temple stands an enormous tree, spreading its branches far and wide; it is ever green, in winter as in summer. No one knows what kind of tree this is. There is also a well there, where heathen sacrifices are commonly performed, and a living man is plunged into it. If he is not found again, it is deemed that the will of the people will be fulfilled."[34]

"A golden chain surrounds the temple, hanging over the gables (fastigia) of the building, glowing brilliantly towards those who approach, for the temple itself stands in a plain, with hills around it in the likeness of a theatre."[35]

"For nine days the festivities with sacrifices of this kind are held. Every day they offer one man together with other animals, so that in nine days it makes seventy-two living things which are sacrificed."[36]

---

[33] Ibid, 1975:244.
[34] Ibid, 1975:245.
[35] Ibid, 1975:245.
[36] Ibid, 1975:245.

I have quoted that in full as it such an intricate and elaborate report. The gory human sacrifices, the thought of just one person killed in sacrifice is abhorrent, never mind nine. As for the sight of seventy-two bodies, I find that totally repugnant, although I realise that life was certainly different then to now, with different standards. Many ancient religions sacrificed animals such as dogs and horses but fewer gave human offerings to the gods.

Adam of Bremen writes that the temple was next to a grove. The grove was seen as sacred and holy by the Norse as it was to many ancient religious creeds. The Celts also considered groves blessed, their priests the Druids conducted rituals in consecrated groves.

Trees were seen as especially hallowed. Adam also writes that the temple was next to a holy evergreen tree. The evergreen ash tree, known as Yggdrasil, was particularly sacred. Yggdrasil was acknowledged to be the World Tree. This holy ash linked all the nine worlds, the whole of Viking creation. Its roots spanned Asgard, which was the home of the Aesir, a group of warrior gods led by Odin, this the world of the gods, similar to heaven; Midgard, the world inhabited by humans; and Niflheim, a land of darkness and freezing mists, the region of Hel. The tree was home to many sacred animals: an eagle, a falcon, a goat, four stags, a squirrel, and a dragon called Nidhogg (who chewed the corpses of evil-doers,) chewed the roots. Here is the description of the animals of Yggdrasil taken from the *Prose Edda*:

> "In the branches of the ash sits an eagle, and it is very knowledgeable, and between the eyes sits a hawk called Vedrfolnir (meaning 'Weather-bleached One'). A squirrel called Ratatosk (meaning 'Gnaw-tooth') springs up and down the ash tree and conveys words of abuse exchanged between the eagle and Nidhogg. Four harts leap about the branches of the ash and eat the shoots; these are their names: Dain, Dvalin, Duneyr, Durathror. And along with Nidhogg in Hvergelmir there are so many serpents that no tongue can count them."[37]

---

[37] The Prose Edda of Snorri Sturluson, Young, 1964:45.

Adam also relates that next to this tree is a holy well. Now that is interesting as in Norse mythology Yggdrasil is associated with a sacred spring called Urd. Near the spring lived three goddesses of destiny, Urd (*Fate*), Verdandi (*Necessity*) and Skuld (*Being*) or put in a different way, Past, Present and Future. They were known as the Norns and decided the fates of men. The Norns drew water from the spring of Urd every day. This water was mixed with the clay of the spring and then sprinkled on the branches of Yggdrasil protecting it from decay. This water was special; it was holy and coloured white. Everything it covered was left with a white film, including Yggdrasil. Here is the *Prose Edda's* description of the white filmed sacred tree:

> *"I know an ash-tree*
> *known as Yggdrasil,*
> *tall tree and sacred*
> *bespent with white clay,*
> *thence come the dews*
> *that fall in the dales;*
> *it stands ever green*
> *over Urd's spring."*[38]

It does sound very similar to the location that Adam described of the pagan temple. The reference to the temple being adorned with gold is also interesting. In Viking mythology there is Valhalla, an immense hall, presided over by the god Odin. It was here that dead warriors, the Einherjar, feasted, fought and awaited Ragnarok. Ragnarok was similar to the Christian concept of Armageddon, an apocalyptic final battle between gods and the giants, when all known life will be destroyed. Valhalla was vast. Here is a portrayal of Valhalla from *The Deluding of Gylfi* in the *Prose Edda* sagas:

---

[38] Ibid, 1964:46.

Figure 4 - Yggdrasil

"I think there are in Valhalla
more than six hundred
and forty doors;
out of a single door at a time
will tramp nine hundred and sixty men,
champions advancing on the monster."[39]

That is a colossal building. But what is particularly fascinating is that this enormous hall is roofed with gilded shields and the pagan temple was depicted as glowing with gold.

Another thing that strikes you with the description of the temple is the likeness to the biblical portrait of the Temple of Solomon:

"Also he made before the house two pillars of thirty and five cubits high, and the chapter that was on the top of each of them was five cubits.
And he made chains, as in the oracle, and put them on the heads of the pillars: and he made an hundred pomegranates, and put them on the chains."[40]

Both buildings had chains. The pagan temple had a golden chain called *'catena'*. But it is a strange detail common to both religious structures.

Adam's account of idols in the temple is echoed in other chronicles. There appeared to be many different idols in ancient Nordic pagan temples. Idols were venerated by the Norse.

There is a wonderful description of one of these idols, an image of the god Thor, god of thunder, given by the Icelandic chronicler Snorri. This statue was huge and decked with gold and silver as befitting a god. It was hollow and standing on a platform. There was a ritual everyday to feed him four loaves and bread and meat. But it is what happened to this statue that is strange. One of St. Olaf's servants struck the idol with a club. Not surprisingly the statue smashed and shattered into many fragments. But the statue was not empty. For out of it poured toads, snakes, and rats, so well fed that they were as big as cats.

---

[39] Ibid, 1964:65.
[40] Chronicles II 3:15-16.

Figure 5 - Valhalla's Gate

The animals had fed on the food. But of course this was an allegory, a parable of the time.

There are other tales of idols. There was an idol of the god Freyr (also called Frey), the god of farming, weather and fertility, in Thrandheim. When the god-king Freyr died in Sweden two wooden men were carved representing the god. These wooden men were known as *tremadr* or 'tree men', and were put into a *howe*, a Scandinavian hollow or hole to keep Freyr company. They were later exhumed and one of them sent to Thrandheim where he was worshipped.

There is another account of Freyr from Sweden which is of interest. It is in the Story of Gunnar Helming. Gunnar Helming fled from Norway and found refuge in the temple of Freyr in Sweden. He placed himself under the protection of Freyr's *'wife'*. There was a ceremony where a statue of Freyr and his bride were carried around on a chariot in a procession through the provinces to ensure fertility for the coming crops and harvest. It was Gunnar's job to lead the horse. But he grew tired of walking and jumped into the chariot. Angered at this sacrilege the idol fell on him and there was a fight between Gunnar and the god. Gunnar thought of King Olaf Tryggvason, a Christian. He called on Christ to help him in his time of need. Now a mighty demon jumped out of the idol. All that was left was a lump of wood. Again this is another parable showing the different traditions of the two religions.

Many images of the gods were considered to become animated and come alive. Some were said to have demons that talked. Sacrifices were made to idols; such was their power and awe. Images were carved into pillars. There is the story of Thorolf Mostrarskegg who cast his pillars into the sea where they sped over the waves safely guiding him to his new abode, where he made his home. Many idols were carved into pillars of temples, on chair posts and on the prows of ships, as homage to the power of the gods. Many mythical scenes were also carved on wood and stone. Some of these have survived in Sweden as magnificent examples of pagan craftsmanship.

The gods mentioned by Adam being worshipped in the temple are Thor, Woden and Fricco. It is commonly thought that Fricco was another name of the Norse god Freyr, a fertility god. Thor was the god of thunder, sky, fertility and the law; Odin was the chief god of the Norse.

There are also stories of how cattle were worshipped as if they were gods. Snorri relates that there was an ancient king who used to sacrifice to a cow. The king would drink the milk from the cow and he took her wherever he went. So attached was he to her that when the cow died the animal was placed in a howe, an ancient hole used as a grave, near to that of the king himself.

This reverence to cows is repeated in another story from the *Ragnars Lodbrokar's Saga*. Ragnar was a pagan who claimed to be a direct descendant of the god Odin. The cow was called Sibilja. The legendary Swedish King, Eysteinn Beli, would worship this cow and called the animal a god. Sibilja was given great sacrifices and revered. She grew fierce and raging. Such was the fear she generated that the animal was placed at the head of the army in battle. Sibilja would roar and the enemy would take flight and fight among each other. Such was the terror of this remarkable cow.

It is a shame that there are not more descriptions of Viking ceremonies. But in *The Deeds of Beowulf* there is a vivid portrayal of a Viking funeral:

> "As for Scyld (Danish Chieftain), he departed, at the destined hour, full of exploit, to go into the Master's keeping. They then carried him forth to the shore of the sea, his faithful comrades, as he himself had requested, while he with his words held sway as lord of the Scyldings; dear chief of the land, he had long tenure of power.
>
> There at the landing-place stood the ship with ringed prow, glistening afresh, and outward bound; convoy for a prince. Down laid they there the beloved chief, dispenser of jewels, on the lap of the ship, the illustrious dead by the mast.
>
> There was store of precious things, ornaments from remote ports, brought together; never heard I of craft comelier fitted with slaughter weapons and campaigning harness, with swords and breast-mail. In his keeping lay a multitude of treasures, which were to pass with him far away into the watery realm.
>
> Not at all with less gifts, less stately opulence, did they outfit him, than those had done, who at the first had sent him forth, lone over the wave, when he was an infant. Furthermore, they set up by him a gold wrought banner, high over his head. They let the flood bear him, gave him over to the ocean; sad was their soul, mourning their mood. Who received that burthen, men,

heads of Halls, heroes under heaven cannot for certain tell. "[41]

You can really picture the sight, the heroic chieftain going to meet the gods. He was obviously successful at raiding. He had accrued many riches. It is interesting just how varied the wealth was. This chieftain had looted many countries carrying back their treasure.

There are also descriptions of Viking funerals by Arab travellers. One of these was Ibn Rustah, a tenth century Persian explorer. He said that when one of the Norse died they are laid in huge graves, the size of a large house. Into these graves are placed meat, drink, money and jewels. But evidently the Norse liked to put everything they liked into the burial tomb. Into the grave also went his favourite wife, still alive. I don't think that I would like to be married in those days, to be buried alive sounds inhuman, not a declaration of love.

Funeral rites differed in relation to the wealth of the deceased. A poor man is placed in a small boat which is then burnt. A rich chieftain however had an elaborate sending off to meet the gods. This was witnessed by another Arab, Ibn Fadlan, a tenth century Muslim writer.

The deceased chieftain's fortune was divided into three. His family had one third, the rest being divided to be used for providing the drink for the mourners attending the funeral, and to buy the equipment which every chief would need in the Otherworld.

Now the man's servants were assembled. They were asked who would like the honour of being buried with their master. It was normally a girl who agreed to die with her master, although sometimes it was a male. This servant was now herself waited upon. But whether she was given attendants to serve her or to stop her escaping is not known.

Now a ship was procured. The body, dressed in all its finery was placed in a tent on the vessel with plenty of food and drink. Now animals were added. A dog was cut in half and placed with his master as well as draught beasts, cows, a cock and a hen.

The girl was passed from man to man who all had intercourse with her. This was done as a symbol of their love for the dead chief. Now the girl was given a hen. She performed a ritual in which the bird's head was cut off and

---

[41] The Saxon Age, Scott, 1979:122.

the head together with the poor unfortunate hen's body was placed in this funeral ship.

An adaptation of this strange rite is the *Tale of Hadding*, son of Gram, King of Denmark. He has many strange adventures, one of which is that he went on a journey underground with a woman. Together they came to a raging river flowing with weapons, then a bridge by which there were many fallen warriors, locked in perpetual battle. Continuing their journey they came to a wall, baring their way. The woman took a cock, tore off its head and threw it over the wall. The cock then came back to life and crowed. There are many symbols of death in this story. In other Norse myths journeys, rivers and bridges symbolise death. Hermod, messenger of the gods, who guided souls to Hades, travels through a torrential river named Gjoll, meaning resounding and one of eleven rivers in the Norse Otherworld, and a bridge on his journey to Hel, the Land of the Dead, where the wicked go. The decapitated cock appears to symbolise life after death, which is consistent with the ritual being used at a Viking funeral.

Other cocks in Norse mythology are related to death. There is the cock called Vidofnir, who sits in the top bough of the sacred ash tree, Yggdrasil. There is also a golden combed cock called Gullinkambi who wakes up the warriors every day in Valhalla, the Land of the Dead where the fallen warriors go. There is as well a cock called Fjalar, the *'All Knower'*. All these birds will crow to the giants and gods at Ragnarok, the end of time. Again more symbolism associating the cock with death.

But back to the funeral, the girl was lifted from the ground three times. The first time she uttered: *"Behold I see my father and mother"*. When lifted again she said: *"I see all my dead relations."* When raised for the last time the girt uttered: *"I see my master seated in Paradise, and Paradise is green and fair... He is calling me, send me to him."*[42] The girl was then placed on the ship and ritually killed by an old woman who was called the *'angel of death'*. She gave her life for her master.

The vessel was now set alight. It and its contents were burnt to ashes. The Chief was now with the gods in the Norse Lands of the Dead. A mound was built over the remains and an inscription was written on it. To the Arab chroniclers these rites were strange. But as a fellow Norse

---

[42] Ibn Fadlan's Travel Report, section 19.

explained, the Arabs were stupid to bury their dead in the ground where the worms would just eat them. To the Norse, the bodies would burn in an instant, leaving the spirit to join the immortals in Viking Paradise, Valhalla.

Of course these ceremonies were disliked by the Christians. Here is a criticism in 1013 CE by the Archbishop of York, Wulfstan in his famous *Sermon of the Wolf to the English, when the Danes were most severely persecuting them*:

> "*In heathen lands one does not dare withhold little nor much of that which is appointed to the worship of false gods; and we withhold everywhere God's dues all too often. And in heathen lands one dares not curtail, within or without the temple, anything brought to the false gods and entrusted as an offering. And we have entirely stripped God's houses of everything fitting, within and without, and God's servants are everywhere deprived of honour and protection. And some men say that no man dare abuse the servants of false gods in any way among heathen people, just as is now done widely to the servants of God*"[43]

Obviously the good archbishop strongly disapproved. Attempts were made to convert the Icelanders and all Norse nations from pagans into good Christians. One of the central figures here was Olaf Tryggvason, king of Norway in 995 CE. He reigned for five years to 1000 CE. In this short period he converted six nations to Christianity, Norway, Iceland, Greenland, Faeroe, Shetland and Orkney; a remarkable achievement for one person.

It is said that Olaf's conversion to Christianity came in a strange manner. On a visit to England he disguised himself and visited a Christian hermit. The hermit saw through the disguise and predicted many things. Olaf was so impressed that he converted to the new religion and was baptised. This was in 994 CE, the year before he became king of Norway.

But when Olaf was in England it was as a violent man, he did not come in peace. With his colleague the Dane, Swein, sometimes written as Sven, Forkbeard he attacked London on the 8th September 994 CE. Here is the description of the raid and the destruction caused in the Laud version of the *Anglo-Saxon Chronicle*:

---

[43] The Electronic Sermo Lupi Ad Anglos, Bernstein, 2004

"In this year of the Nativity of St Mary (8th September) came Anlaf (Olaf) and Swein (Sven Forkbeard) to London with ninety-four ships, and kept up an unceasing attack on the city, and they purposed moreover, to set it on fire, but there they suffered greater loss and injury than they ever thought possible that any garrison would inflict upon them. But in this (day) the holy Mother of God manifested her clemency to the garrison and delivered them from their foes. They went away doing as much harm as any host (enemy) was capable of doing in burning, harrying and slaughter, both along the coast and in Essex, Kent, Sussex, and Hampshire."[44]

He appeared to have a long way to go before becoming a good Christian, with all that killing and bloodshed. King Ethelred the Redeless had to buy peace from the plundering Viking. It cost the then staggering amount of 16,000 pounds of silver. Olaf now promised never to attack England again. Perhaps there was no money left to make it worth his while. What is odd now though is that King Ethelred stood sponsor for Olaf to be confirmed into the Christian religion. I would have thought that with Olaf's bloodthirsty record this would have been denied. But when Olaf became King of Norway in 995 CE he took with him a Christian bishop, called either Jon or Sigurd, records vary, and some priests. The conversion of the pagan Vikings had begun.

Even though Olaf was said to have returned to Norway and converted the inhabitants, there were still pockets of Paganism. In a story dated about the late twelfth to early thirteenth centuries in the codex *Flateyjarbok* there is a reference to pagan temples and the Christian King. Evidently the King entered a temple at Mearin in Thrandlheim. In this temple were many images of the old Norse pagan gods. In the centre of these images was a representation of the great god Thor: *"he was of enormous size, and worked all over in gold and silver. This is how Thor was arranged: he was sitting in a chariot, a very splendid one, and two wooden goats, finely carved, were harnessed before it.. .."*[45] It must have been a spectacular sight, seeing Thor in all his finery. The temple was probably still in use, as although Olaf converted the

---

[44] The Anglo-Saxon Chronicle, Garmonsway (trans), 1975:127.
[45] Myth and Religion of the North, Turnville-Petre, 1975:82.

country to Christendom, there were still had many pagan countryman who kept to the old ways.

There is another story that confirms this theory. The Icelandic poet Hallfred, who was now said to be a good Christian, came before the court of the Christian King Olaf Tryggvason. His crime was that he kept an ivory image of the god Thor in his purse that he worshipped secretly. I would have thought that this was quite common in those days.

It is likely that when Olaf returned to Norway he preached Christianity like he had raided England, with fire and sword. Anyway he died after his personal vessel was ambushed in the Baltic by a jarl, a Danish nobleman called Eirik in battle between him and his enemy the Danes. This magnificent ship the 'Long Serpent', was a truly grand vessel so large that it needed thirty four oars a side to man it and was the most powerful ship in the northern waters. Olaf, vastly outnumbered against the Danes, put up a heroic fight. He was a dazzling figure standing on the prow of his ship, resplendent in a scarlet cloak. But Olaf leapt overboard and disappeared under the waves; thus died one of Norway's most remarkable rulers. However Olaf was a strong swimmer, and as with so many heroes there were stories that he was still alive, that he had been rescued and was seen in many countries including the Holy Land. As Snorri said: *"Be that as it may, King Olaf never again returned to his kingdom in Norway"*.[46]

It is interesting that there are different accounts of Olaf Tryggvason depending on either the Norwegian or Icelandic writers. These stem from the different interpretations of the Danish historian, Saxo Grammatiicus. Saxo was probably born around 1150 CE. Not much is known about him apart from the fact that he was the secretary of Absalon, who was Bishop of Roskilde 1158 CE and Archbishop of Lund 1178-1201 CE. Saxo relates that Absalon himself asked him write his monumental work. This comprised the *Gesta Danorum*, sixteen books in Latin, chronicling the history of the Danes from prehistoric times to the late twelfth century. A massive and important work, though it must be pointed out that as with many early histories it was based on folktales and oral tradition. These were mainly from west Norse tradition with some of it from Danish folklore. So it is not as historically accurate as modern histories. But it still provides an

---

[46] A History of the Vikings, Jones, 1994:139.

important source of knowledge for the history of the Norse peoples.

To the Icelanders and the Norwegians, Olaf Tryggvason was a hero who began the conversion of Norway to Christendom. His Danish opponent Sven Forkbeard was a villain. Evidently Olaf had a choice of two brides, the widowed Swedish queen, Sigrid and Sven's sister Thyri. Olaf refused Sigrid because she refused to recant her pagan beliefs and become Christian. He therefore married Thyri. By marrying Thyri he was entitled to lands and in attempting to recover these terrains which were rightfully his he was attacked by Sven. This led to his death in battle by the Danes in 1000 CE.

The Danes did not see him like this at all. To them Olaf was stupid, brutal and untrustworthy. Olaf was now the aggressor. Sven had tricked him, and deprived him of 'two most splendid matches'; that of Sigrid and Thyri, now Sven's daughter. Olaf wanted revenge.

The last battles are the same between Olaf and Sven. Olaf was still killed. But apart from that the story is totally different. I will leave it to you to see who you believe.

There is a nice description of Olaf Tryggvason by Adam of Bremen in his work *Gesta Hammaburgensis ecclesiae pontificum*. This task was completed just before 1075 CE. Even here there is differences in Olaf's role to Christianity. First he says that Olaf *"was the first to bring Christianity to his fatherland"*.[47] He then describes what seem to be many pagan attributes:

> *"some relate that Olaf had been a Christian, some that he had forsaken Christianity; all, however, affirm that he was skilled in divination, was an observer of the lots,. And had placed all his hope in the prognostication of birds. Wherefore, also he received a byname, so that he was called Craccaben. In fact they say that he was also given to the practice of the magic art and supported as his household companions all the magicians with whom that land was overrun, and, deceived by their error perished."*[48]

Obviously Olaf was an enigmatic figure who while supporting Christianity did not forget his pagan origins or how those magical arts could be put to use.

---

[47] Kings and Vikings, Sawyer, 1982:18.
[48] Ibid, 1982:18.

Although it was Olaf Tryggvason who started the conversion of the Norwegians to Christianity, his work was completed by a later king of Norway, Olaf Haraldson (995-1030 CE) who later became St Olaf. Olaf was the half brother of Harald III of Norway, so he had royal blood in him. But true to the times of the age he became a Viking mercenary at the age of twelve. He then raided many countries, including Frisia, Normandy, Spain, and England. The attack on England is interesting in that it included an assault on London. London Bridge was pulled down by grappling irons.

In Prof. Sawyers book *The Age of the Vikings* there is an extract from the Saga of St. Olaf by Snorri describing how Olaf took his ships under London Bridge:

> *"wound cables round the stakes which supported the bridge, and, taking the cables, they rowed all the ships downstream as hard as ever they could. The stakes were dragged along the bottom until they were loosened under the bridge ... and the bridge came crashing down and many fell into the river ... Now when the citizens saw that the River Thames was won, so that they could no longer prevent the ships from pressing up inland, they were stricken with terror at the advance of the ships, and gave up the city and accepted King Ethelred."*[49]

But putting his pagan past behind him, Olaf converted to Christianity in 1013 CE. He became King of Norway two years later in 1015 CE taking the throne from Erik and Svend Jarl.

There is a very odd story concerning Olaf in the *Story of Volsi*. During these far off times customs were very different to today. To the ancient pagan people sacrifices were common, given to appease the gods. Horses were frequently used. After being sacrificed the unfortunate animal was eaten. Its liver was considered particularly sacred and consumed. But this particular story concerns a different part of the horse's anatomy.

The story relates to the pagan practices of an old man and his wife who lived in isolated area in the north of Norway. Paganism despite many attempts to eradicate it still was prevalent in the heartland of the country, especially with the rural population. This couple had a son, daughter, thrall and serving-maid. One autumn the family's fat draught-

---

[49] The Age of the Vikings, Sawyer, 1971:40.

horse died. The animal was skinned and stewed ready to eat. The farmer's son took the horse's penis called '*vingull*' and ran into the house shaking the organ in front of the women chanted:

"Here you can see
a good stout vingull
chopped off from the horse's father.

For you, serving-maid,
this Volsi (phallus) will be
lively enough
between the thighs.[50]

The farmer's wife grasped the vingull. She said that she didn't like to see anything wasted. The organ was preserved, it was dried and wrapped in a linen cloth, with onions and herbs to preserve it and put it into her chest. Here I must say it sounds as if she was making jam or marmalade rather than preserving a penis. But the vingull became a magic symbol. Every evening she would intone a magical chant. It became her own god (*gud sinn*). Soon the whole family were offering prayers to it. It was said that the vingull became so powerful that it could stand beside the housewife. The ritual continued every evening. Verses were chanted by each member of the family.

Late one evening Olaf arrived at the household. He came accompanied with Finn Arnason and the Icelandic poet, Thormod. Olaf and his friends were horrified by the ritual. They seated themselves in the hall waiting for the household to assemble. The last member of the family to enter was the housewife who brought the vingull. It now had its own name, Volsi. Volsi was passed from hand to hand. When held a verse usually obscene was uttered over it. There was always, though, the same ending to the verse:

"May Mornir
receive this sacrifice."

The royal party were totally horrified by the whole ceremony. Unfortunately we do not know who Mornir was. There are many theories as to the origin of this word. There is a suggestion that perhaps Mornir was the name of a fertility goddess, possibly Skadi, the '*goddess of snow-shoes*', wife of the fertility god Njord. '*Mornir*' can also be a name for

---

[50] Myth and Religion of the North, Turnville-Petre, 1975:256.

a sword. Or perhaps Mornir was just another name for phallus. Who now knows?

Olaf was very zealous in his attempts to convert the country into Christianity. Paganism was to be exterminated with fire and the sword. This made him very unpopular with his subjects, many of whom still followed the old ways of paganism. King Cnut (Canute), who was king of Denmark from 1014 CE, and was crowned king of England three years later in 1017 CE, invaded Norway in 1028 CE. The people rebelled against Olaf's tyranny. He fled to the court of his brother-in-law, Jaroslav of Russia. Jaroslav gave him 4000 men to regain his throne. He met his rival Cnut in battle at Stiklastoadir in 1030 CE in a valiant attempt to recover his country, but he was defeated and slain. Here is the Parker version of the *Anglo-Saxon Chronicle*, describing those years:

> *"1028. In this year king Cnut sailed from England to Norway with fifty ships, and drove King Olaf from that country, and secured possession of all of it for himself. 1029. In this year Cnut returned home to England. 1030. In this year king Olaf returned to Norway, and the people united to oppose him and fought against him, and he was there slain."*[51]

There is a wonderful story about Olaf's last battle at Stiklastoadir in 1030 CE. Many adventurers and criminals flocked to join his army. Two of these who were highwaymen and robbers, Afra-Fasti and Gauka-Thorir, led a band of thirty men to join Olaf in battle. They asked the king if they could enlist. Olaf enquired: *"are you Christian?"* They replied that they were neither Christian nor Heathen, but still wanted to fight on his side. This was not good enough for Olaf who said they must first be baptised. They both refused, although they followed the army at a distance. It is interesting that Olaf did not seem to mind that they were highwaymen and robbers, only that they were not Christians.

Heathenism was common in the army. When the king reached the battlefield he found that there were over a thousand pagans in his troops. A mass baptism was called but many refused and left. Now Afra-Fasti and Gauka-Thorir came forward to offer their services but still they refused to be baptised. The robbers talked among as to what they should do. One said: *"I shall join in the battle, giving support*

[51] The Anglo-Saxon Chronicle, Garmonsway (trans), 1975:156.

to one side or the other; it does not matter to me on which side I fight." The other robber was principled and decided to fight for the king. But he added: *"if I have to believe in a god, why should it be worse for me to believe in the White Christ than any other?"* His friend was won over and persuaded to support Olaf. Both now took baptism. The story provides an illustration of religion in those days.

Surprisingly for a king who was unpopular and overthrown, he was made a saint and became patron saint of Norway in 1164 CE. His body was taken to the cathedral of Trondheim. Here many miracles occurred ensuring his canonisation. The feast day of St. Olaf is 29th July.

But King Canute in England also enforced Christianity. In *Laws of Cnut*, in the *English Historical Documents, Vol. 1* there is a law prohibiting heathen practice. This dates from 1020-1023 CE:

> *"5. And we earnestly forbid every heathen practice.*
> *It is heathen practice if one worships idols, namely if one worships heathen gods and the sun or the moon, fire or flood, wells or stones or any kind of forest trees, or if one practises witchcraft or encompasses death by any means, either by sacrifice or divination, or takes part in such delusions."*[52]

Thus in England the ancient pagan religions were banned; although the memories of the older gods remained in such things as the names of the days of the week, with each one symbolising a deity or object of pagan worship.

---

[52] English Historical Documents 500-1042, Whitelock, 1979:455.

PART 3
BEGINNINGS AND ENDINGS

THE NORSE STORY OF CREATION

Before we look more deeply into the days of the week and the gods that they were associated with, it would be interesting and informative to our understanding of the Viking attitude to time if we look at the mythology of Norse creation. The story of the beginning of the world is found in Snorri Sturluson's *The Prose Edda*. In answer to the important questions: *"What is the origin of all things? How did they begin? What existed before?"*[53] The *Edda* gives the following reply:

> *"In the beginning*
> *not anything existed,*
> *there was no sand nor sea*
> *nor cooling waves;*
> *earth was unknown*
> *and heaven above*
> *only Ginnungagap*
> *was - there was no grass"*[54]

Ginnungagap was a void. It was a deep yawning gulf, so deep in fact that the human eye could not see to the bottom. This great abyss was enveloped in perpetual twilight.

It is interesting that the Norse myths have the start of creation as a void, with little light, only perpetual twilight. In the Classical tradition of the Greeks and Romans it related that in the beginning the world was a confused mass. The Earth as we know it did not exist. There was just formless Chaos, with no light.

Here is the Latin poet Ovid's (43BCE – 17CE) description of the Greek and Roman creation of the world:

> *"Before the seas, and this terrestrial ball,*
> *And Heav'n's high canopy, that covers all,*
> *One was the face of Nature; if a face:*
> *Rather a rude and indigested mass:*
> *A lifeless lump, unfashion'd, and unfram'd,*

---

[53] The Prose Edda of Snorri Sturluson, Young, 1964:32.
[54] Ibid, 1964:32.

Of jarring seeds; and justly Chaos nam'd.
No sun was lighted up, the world to view;
No moon did yet her blunted horns renew:
Nor yet was Earth suspended in the sky,
Nor pois'd, did on her own foundations lye:
Nor seas about the shores their arms had thrown;
But earth, and air, and water, were in one.
Thus air was void of light, and earth unstable,
And water's dark abyss unnavigable."[55]

There appear to be similarities between that and the Norse version of the void of the main part of the land of Ginnungagap.

But Ginnungagap consisted of two very distinct regions. In the north there was the land of Niflheim, a world of darkness and freezing mist. Directly opposite Niflheim was the land of Muspell, a world of fire and heat.

Iceland, where the creation myth in Snorri's *Edda* originated, is a land of distinct contrasts. It is a land of seething volcanoes spurting hot lava and freezing icy mist and glaciers. In the summer there are endless days of light and in the winter unending darkness. The lands of Niflheim and Muspell recreate these extreme conditions that would have been very familiar to the Icelandic people. Here is a description of the topography of Iceland made by William Jackson Hooker, F.L.S. in the *Journal of a Tour in Iceland in the summer of 1809*:

> *"Imagine to yourself an island, which from one end to the other presents to your view only barren mountains, whose summits are covered with eternal snow, and between them fields divided by vitrified cliffs, whose high and sharp points seem to vie with each other to deprive you of the sight of a little grass which scantily springs up among them...Rivers and fresh-water lakes abound; the latter of very considerable extent and well supplied with fish; the former... much obstructed by rocks and shallows."*[56]

---

[55] Metamorphoses, Ovid, 1.7-20.
[56] Journal of a Tour in Iceland in the Summer of 1809, Hooker, 1811:lix.

Considering the northern region of Niflheim first, this was a land of icy cold fog, snow and darkness. In death wicked men would go to Hel and from there to Niflheim. It was not a nice place. It lay with the land of Hel in the bottom of Yggdrasil, the sacred ash, among the lowest part of the roots of the magical tree.

In the centre of Niflheim there was a well called Hvergelmir, 'the Bubbling Cauldron'.

This was the source of eleven rivers called the Elivager ('ice-waves'). These rivers all had names describing their different temperaments. There was Svol, the cool river; Gunnthra, the battle defiant one; Fjorm, and Fimbulthul, the loud bubbling waters; Slid, the fearsome river; Hriod, the storming one; Sylg, Ylg, and Vid, the broad rivers; Leipt, the fast as lightning waters; and the freezing Gjoll. Gjoll was situated right next to Hel's gate. The Elivager was a mighty torrent of gushing water. But it was located in the freezing cold land of Niflheim. The waters all turned to huge blocks of ice which surged down into the dark, bleak, deep abyss, with a mighty thunder like roar. But perhaps it is better left to the *Eddas* for the most graphic description of this mighty river:

> *"When those rivers which are called Elivager came so far from their source that the yeasty venom accompanying them hardened like slag, it turned into ice. Then when that ice formed and was firm, a drizzling rain that arose from the venom poured over it and cooled into rime, and one layer of ice. Formed on top of the other throughout Ginnungagap."*[57]

This story of a torrent of water is echoed in classical Greek and Roman myths. They had a mighty river called Oceanus. This surged in a circle around the edge of the world. It was also a special river, for from it flowed all the seas, lakes, rivers and springs. In this it was similar to Elivager from which all those rivers flowed.

The land of Muspell directly opposite the land of Niflheim was totally different in character. This was a land of fire, light and heat. It was so hot that those who were not native to the land could not endure it. Muspell was the home of the fire giant, Surt. Surt was married to another giantess,

---

[57] The Prose Edda of Snorri Sturluson, Young, 1964:33.

Sinmora. This giant has a flaming sword, which constantly sends forth showers of sparks. This frightening creature will be there at the end of the world and will vanquish all gods and burn the whole universe with fire. A terrifying thought. Here is Snorri's description of that fateful time:

"Surt from the south comes
with the spoiler of twigs (fire)
blazing his sword
(like) sun of the Mighty Ones;
mountains will crash down,
troll-women stumble,
men tread the road to Hel,
heaven's rent asunder."[58]

As the hazy heat of Muspell met the freezing cold frost of Niflheim in Ginnungagap, the frost thawed and dripped, and layer by layer, the likeness of a man appeared. This became a giant called Ymir. He was a frost ogre. But those drops of frost were poisonous and the giant became evil. The frost ogres called him Aurgelmir meaning 'Mud Seether', a very descriptive title. Here is Seamund's Edda, the Henderson translation, description of the world at that time:

"In early times,
When Ymir lived,
Was sand, nor sea,
Nor cooling wave;
No earth was found
Nor heaven above;
One chaos all,
And nowhere grass."[59]

This seems to me to be very like Ovid's Greek description of the beginning of the world and Chaos.

Ymir fell asleep. While he slept he began to sweat. Under his left arm there grew a man and a woman. From his legs there came sons, one from each foot. One of his sons was a six headed giant called Thrudgelmir, the 'Mighty Roarer'. An apt name considering that he had six throats and six tongues. He would certainly have made an ear-splitting

---

[58] The Prose Edda of Snorri Sturluson, Young, 1964:89.
[59] The Norsemen (Myths and Legends), Guerber, 1994:9.

noise. Thrudgelmir, in turn beget the giant Bergelmir. These giants appear to be hermaphrodite, giving birth to both men and women from their own body without the aid of female assistance. This was the start of the family of frost ogres.

There is a parallel to this story in Persian mythology. Here Ahura Mazda, god of light and lord of knowledge is opposed by Angra Mainyu, an evil spirit and god of darkness sometimes known as Ahriman. Like Ymir he created people from sweat. Gayomart was constructed in this manner. Gayomart was the first man, another parallel with Ymir. He was destroyed by the wicked Angra Mainyu. But it is from Gayomart that there came the human race. He had twin children, Mashya and Mashyane who became the first human beings. These children were born in the shape of trees, closely entwined. But Ahura Mazda spoke to them, ordering: *"Be human beings and bring forth the race of mankind!"* This creation legend was also common to the Zoroastrian faith

More frost thawed and solidified. This time a cow was created called Audhumla, *'the Nourisher'*. Ymir now had a supply of sustenance. From the cow's udder flowed four great rivers of milk. The giant would never get hungry.

Audhumla herself had to eat. She sought the salt from the ice and began to lick it with her rough tongue. By the evening of the first day a man's hair appeared from the ice. Audhumla continued to lick the ice blocks. On the second day a whole head emerged. By the end of the third day a whole man had appeared. This was Buri, a name meaning *'producer'*.

Buri was strong and handsome. He produced a son called Bor, the name having the meaning *'born'*. Bor married the giantess Bestla, a daughter of the giant Bolthorn, signifying the thorn of evil. Bestla and Bor had three children, all strong sons. The first was Odin, meaning *'spirit'*, the second Vili, meaning *'will'*, and the third son was Ve, meaning *'holy'*.

It is interesting that we have Audhumla, the cow giving the first men food. Cows, as milk-producers generally are symbols of Mother Earth. In the ancient Egyptian religion cows had a special importance. There is the Egyptian goddess of creation, Nuit. She is often depicted as a celestial cow stretching across the sky, held aloft by the air god Shu.

Nuit was often seen as the goddess of the sky. The worship of Nuit dates back to approx. 3000 BCE.

Hathor, the Egyptian goddess was often depicted with a cows head or sometimes as an actual cow. She was the goddess of love and beauty. She was a mother goddess and was mother of all Egyptian pharaohs. In fact, the pharaoh was known as *'son of Hathor'*. Hathor represented fertility as does the cow. She was a very popular goddess and was worshipped from 2700 BCE.

The cow's horns are often depicted as a crescent. This is associated with the horn of plenty, and the moon. In Sumer the cow itself was often represented as a crescent moon. Here the starry night is described as: *"dominated by the mighty Bull whose fertile cow is the Full Moon, and whose herd is the Milky Way."*[60] The night sky in Sumer appears to have been dominated by cattle.

Cows, of course, are sacred in Hinduism. The animal is treated with the utmost reverence and respect. It is not killed. Here it is seen as representing the ideals of non violence, known as *ahimsa*. This is one of the goals of motherhood and characterises the ideals of the Mother Goddess. There are five products attained from the cow; milk, clarified butter, curds, urine and dung. These are all seen as purifying and used, with small amounts consumed, in rituals. They also form an important and practical part of Hindu life. Milk, clarified butter and curds are eaten as part of the diet. Cow urine is seen as a cleansing agent, although I think I would prefer to use soap. Dried dung is used as an important fuel.

But I digress, back to Bor and his three sons. There was animosity between Bor's family and the frost ogres. Odin, Vili and Ve attacked and killed their foe, Ymir. The giant was mortally wounded and as he fell he bled profusely. The blood flowed in a torrent, so much blood that there was a deluge which turned into a flood. All the race of frost ogres drowned, apart from one. This was the giant Bergelmir who escaped with his family in a boat made from a hollowed out tree trunk. He went to the land of Jotunheim, the home of the giants. Here he made his home and conceived a new race

---

[60] The Penguin Dictionary of Symbols, Chevalier & Gheerbrant, 1996.

of frost giants who were all hostile to the territory of the gods which they had to leave in such a harsh manner.

It is interesting to compare this Norse myth of a deluge with the flood, with Bergelmir being Noah. Certainly both escaped in a form of craft. But here the similarities stop. Noah was definitely a man, Bergelmir was a giant and the flood waters in the Viking version appear to be from blood rather than water. Although I do have to say that tales of a deluge are very common in all forms of mythology. There are over five hundred World Flood myths from both eastern and western hemispheres, including those from Babylon, India, Russia, Indonesia, New Guinea, the Mojave Apache Indians from North America and the Sherente in South America. It is a very widespread parable in many cultures.

The sons of Bor took the body of the giant Ymir on their shoulders and carried it to the centre of the abyss of Ginnungagap. The world was made from the corpse of the dead giant. His blood became the seas and lakes, his flesh the earth. His unbroken bones became mountains and his teeth, jaws and shattered bones, made rocks and pebbles. Thus the universe was created.

There was so much blood in the giant that there was enough to fashion the ocean. This was placed around the earth. This ocean was so wide that is was impossible to cross it.

All the parts of Ymir were used. His skull was taken and made into the sky. This was placed above the earth and sea. The sky reached to the four corners of the earth. In each corner there was a dwarf called East, West, North and South. These dwarves held the sky in place on their shoulders. Thus the compass points got their name. The giant's brains became the clouds in the sky.

Sparks and glowing embers had been blown from the hot land of Muspell. These were thrown high into the sky and became stars, which gave light to the heavens and earth below.

The most brilliant of these sparks became the sun and the moon. But who should direct these two orbs? The giant Mundilfari had two very beautiful children, Mani, the moon and Sol the sun. The sun and moon were placed in beautiful golden chariots. Mani and Sol were directed by the gods to guide their carriages in the sky. These special chariots have

Figure 6 – Ymir

mystical horses harnessed to them. These are Arvakr, the *'early waker'*, and Allsvin, the *'rapid goer'*. The horses were protected from the heat of the sun by iron cold bellows placed under their shoulder blades to keep them cool. They were also given the protection of the magical shield Svalin, *'the cooler'*. This shield was placed in front of the carriage to shelter the animal from the heat of the sun's rays, otherwise the creatures would have been burned to a cinder. The moon's chariot was pulled by a horse called Alsvider, *'the all swift'*. This animal did not need a special shield, as the moon's rays were a lot cooler than those of the sun.

Mani, the moon was accompanied by two children who had been snatched from earth. These were Huiki, the waxing moon, and Bil, the waning moon. The children had been forced by a cruel father to carry water all night. To the Norse, these children could be seen on the moon, like Jack and Jill, carrying their pail of water. This was similar to Europeans seeing the face of a man on the moon.

But to the ancients evil always trod after good, trying to destroy it. The sun and moon were constantly chased by fierce wolves out to destroy them and plunge the world into darkness. The wolf called Skoll, *'repulsion'*, ran after the sun and the wolf called Hati, *'hatred'*, chased the moon. Every so often the wolves overtook and tried to swallow their prey. This resulted in an eclipse. The sight of an eclipse alarmed the people who would shout and scream in terror. This would cause the wolves to drop their quarry. Light returned.

The wolves were the sons of an old giantess who lived in Iron Wood, which was in the east of Midgard. This aged giantess gave birth to many giant sons, all in the shape of wolves. The most powerful of these was called Managarm, or *'Moon's Dog'*. This beast was said to gorge on the flesh of all those who die. One day he will swallow the moon and spatter the sky and the air with blood. Then the sun will dim and the wind will become wild and violent. Wolves were thought to be able to see in the dark. Thus they are important in legends about the sun and moon. Wolves have been symbolic of the savage in many ancient myths.

Now was the time to create night and day. Nott or Night came from a giant called Narfi, and was his daughter, a dark and swarthy girl. Night married three times. The first to Naglfari, they had a son called Aud. Her second marriage was to Annar, with whom she had a daughter called Jord, 'Earth'. Her last marriage was to Dellinger, 'Dawn', the Shining One, one of the family of gods. They produced the bright and beautiful Day.

Odin took Night and her son Day and placed them in horse drawn chariots like those of the sun and moon. These chariots rode around the world every twenty four hours. Night's chariot was pulled by a horse called Hrimfaxi, 'frosty mane'. It was from Hrimfaxi's waving mane that the dew and hoar-frost dropped down on to earth. Day's horse was called Skinfaxi, meaning 'shining mane', this horse could illuminate the sky, bringing light and gladness to all. The night was colder than the day, and the day lighter than the night.

The gods now had Sun, Moon, Day and Night attending the earth. But to divide the days further they commissioned guardians: Evening, Midnight, Morning, Forenoon, Noon, and Afternoon to assist them.

According to Norse myth there were only two seasons, Summer and Winter. Summer was warm and gentle. The season was a son of the god Svasud, the mild and lovely. Everyone loved Summer except Winter, his deadly enemy. Winter was the son of Vindaul and the grandson of Vasud, both pretty nasty deities. Vasud was the freezing icy wind. That was why winter was a lot colder and more inhospitable than summer.

The winds were controlled by a huge giant called Hreasvelgr, whose name means 'the corpse swallower'; which shows how the Norse viewed winds. He came from the extreme north of the heavens. Hreasvelgr was in the shape of the eagle. When he flapped his enormous wings there were sweeping icy blasts of freezing cold air.

The frost giant Ymir's flesh had become riddled with maggots. These maggots developed into dwarves. They were dark, treacherous and cunning creatures. These dwarves inhabited the land of Svartalfheim, the Land of the Dark Elves. They were also known as dwarves, trolls, gnomes, or kobolds.

Figure 7 - Skoll & Hati

These little folk lived underground. They collected gold, silver and precious stones and were gifted metal smiths who made many magical weapons. Among these mysterious items were the spear point of Odin's spear Gungnir, which was made from the wood of the mystical ash tree Yggdrasil with magical runes carved on it by Odin himself. This weapon never failed in its aim. They made the ship Skidbladnir, a truly special vessel, it would always sail to favourable winds, in fact it did not need to sail in water at all, it could also travel in the air. Furthermore, this remarkable vessel could be folded up until it was small enough to fit in your pocket. Other items constructed were Thor's magic hammer Mjollnir and Odin's ring Draupnir.

People had to beware; they were mischievous and delighted in stealing women and children. They would emerge from the deep recesses of the earth to torment folk and give them nightmares. There were also associated with disease. In Norway, the term 'alvskot', from the word for elves is applied to certain illnesses of man and beast. In Iceland there is a form of skin disease in animals called 'alfabruni', or 'elf-burn'.

Dwarves were also said to have great wisdom and were also masters of runes and magic songs. Living underground they could not face the sun; they were turned to stone by the sun's rays.

The maggots also grew into more pleasant creatures. These elves were fair, good and friendly. They were called Fairies and Elves. Totally different from the dark underground dwarves of Svartalfheim, these little people lived in the air, between heaven and earth in the land of Alfheim, home of light elves. These were more nature spirits. They loved flowers, plants and butterflies and would dance, often in circles, in the light of the moon. In fact they often glided down to earth on a moonbeam.

These elves, known as fairies in England were specially associated with music and dancing. There circular dances known as fairy rings were magical. If a man stood in the middle of one of these according to Scandinavian myth he would die. Interestingly if the same thing happened in England the man would be blessed. Their music was also special with magical properties. Anyone hearing it would dance. They could not stop and would continue to dance until they dropped down dead.

Figure 8 - Alfheim

The name elves come from the same root as the Latin word for white, *'albus'*. It is from albus that you have the name Alps, for those wonderful snow capped mountains. Also the old name for England, Albion, also has the same root. This was because the white cliffs of what is now Dover could be seen from afar.

There were many dwarves all with their own name. We have already heard of those named after the compass points. Here are some others with the translations of their name: Althjof, Dvalin, *'One lying in a trance'*; Nar, *'Corpse'*; Nain, Iping, Dain, Bilfur, Bombor, Nori, *'raging one'*; Onar, Oin, Mjodvitnir, *'Mead wolf'*; Vig, Gandalf, *'Sorcerer elf'*; Vinndalf, *'Wind Elf'*; and Thorin, the *'Bold One'*. There are others, in the *Edda* there is a large list of them. But their leader and the most famous was called Modsognir, his deputy was Durin.

In Scandinavia and Germany sacrifices were made to Elves. This was known as Alfablot. There is the story of a severely wounded man who offered the elves a sacrifice of an ox. The animal was ritually killed on the duelling field. The blood of the beast was smeared on a mound which was inhabited by elves and the meat left for the elf. The man was now healed of his injury. Other sacrifices offered were small animals, or less gory, a bowl of honey and milk.

It was thought that not only did elves heal, but they could also bring prosperity to families. This practice was stopped by the Christian missionaries, who taught that the elves were demons.

The elves, both light and dark, were seen as household gods. They, with other Norse gods and heroes, were carved into the doorposts. These doorposts were taken with the Norse on their ships. When deciding where to land and make a home, the doorposts were cast overboard. Where the waves carried was where the Northmen landed. They trusted their household gods to show them to favourable place to inhabit.

The earth was now round. This is in ancient Norse mythology. It took modern civilisation a long while to agree with the *Eddas* that the earth was circular. The earth was now surrounded by sea. But there was hostility from the giants of Jotunheim. To protect their land the sons of Bor took Ymir's eyebrows and made them into bulwarks and ramparts. This they put round their own section of land and called this land Midgard.

Here is the original description of the creation of earth from the *Eddas*:

> *"From Ymir's flesh*
> *the earth was made*
> *and from his blood the sea,*
> *crags from his bones,*
> *trees from his hair,*
> *and from his skull the sky.*
>
> *From his eyebrows*
> *the blessed gods*
> *made Midgard for the sons of men,*
> *and from his brains*
> *were created*
> *all storm-threatening clouds."*[61]

But there were still no people, only gods, dwarves, and giants. The gods had created Midgard for man. The three sons of the god Bor; Odin, Vili, and Ve, were walking along the seashore. Here they found two fallen trees, an ash and an elm. It was from these trees that the first man and woman were created. Each of these gods donated something special to mankind. From Odin there were the gifts of spirit and life. Vili gave them the gifts of understanding and the power of movement. From Ve there were the gifts of form, speech, hearing and sight. Thus mankind was equipped for life and living in the universe. They had the power to love, hope, and work; the human race could now live and die. They were now given clothes and names. The ash was called Ask, and the elm Embla.

The Human race now inhabited the land of Midgard. Gradually they populated it. It was from this that all the different nations and races of men originated. The gods, having created mankind, looked over them, giving them aid when needed and protected them.

The gods built Asgard, the home of the gods, to dwell in. This was a wonderful place of green plains, a splendid

---

[61] The Prose Edda of Snorri Sturluson, Young, 1964:35.

palace. It was situated high over Midgard, similar to the Christian Heaven. Here there were twelve gods, known as the Aesir, the guardians of man.

An enormous building was built in Asgard. This was a very beautiful building, it glistened like gold. According to the *Edda* it was: *"the largest and best dwelling on earth."*[62] Inside there were thrones for the twelve gods. This residence was called Gladsheim, meaning *'Radiant Home'*. Other grand halls were erected. A sanctuary to the goddess, another very magnificent building, called Vingolf, meaning *'Friendly Floor'*.

Now they erected a well equipped workshop and forge. From this they fashioned many items from metals, stone and wood. But it was gold that was most used by the gods. All household utensils and furniture were constructed from this precious metal. No wonder this age was called the Golden Age.

There were other magnificent halls in Asgard. The son of Odin called Baldur, the Beautiful, resided at Breidablik , meaning *'Gleaming far and wide'*. Baldur was a sun god, he radiated beams of sunshine. He was the god of innocence and light. His palace matched his reputation. It had a silver roof which rested upon golden pillars. So pure was this dwelling that nothing common or unclean was allowed inside.

The son of Baldur, Foresti, lived a palace called Glitnir, meaning *'Radiant Place'*. Foresti was the lawgiver, he was god of justice and righteousness. Glitnir was a magnificent residence. It had a silver roof and walls, posts and pillars made from red gold. Such was its brilliance that it could be seen from a great distance.

There was also the palace of Himinbjorg, meaning *'Mount of Heaven'*. This was situated at the end of Asgard by the rainbow bridge that joined Asgard to Midgard, the land of men. This was the home of Heimdall. Heimdall was a god of light. He was always depicted in white armour. Heimdall had gold teeth and had the surname Gullintani meaning *'golden toothed'*. He had a special horse called Goldtuft.

---

[62] The Prose Edda of Snorri Sturluson, Young, 1964:40.

Figure 9 - Heimdall

Heimdall was the guardian and warden of Asgard, and sat at the end of heaven to guard the bridge from the cliff giants. He had the special power of being able to see a hundred leagues in front of him by night as well as by day. His hearing was so sensitive that he could hear the grass growing. Thus he was gifted to carry out his important duties of making sure that Heaven was protected. Heimdall also had the gift of a magical trumpet called Giallar-horn. This instrument sounded a mellow note whenever a god arrived on the bridge on his way to Asgard. But at the end of the world, which the Norse called Ragnarok, this horn would sound a terrible blast announcing this dreadful event.

Then there was the palace of Valaskjalf, meaning 'Hall of the slain'. Here Vali lived with his father, Odin. Valaskjalf was another remarkable building; its roof was made from silver. Vali was a god of eternal light and love. Arrows are symbolic of beams of light, and Vali was depicted as an archer. It is interesting to note that this god is designated a month in the Norwegian calendar. This is called Lios-beri, the 'light-bringing'. It falls between the middle of January and February. During this period there is the Christian calendar Valentine's Day. St. Valentine was like Vali the patron of lovers.

The throne of Odin, called Hlidskialf, was in the hall of Valaskjalf. This was a magical seat situated high in Asgard. When seated in it, Odin could survey the whole world. He could see at a glance all that was happening among gods, giants, elves, dwarves and men. He could view the whole planet.

In the southern end of Asgard is the palace called Gimle meaning 'Lee of fire'. This was the most beautiful hall of all. It was brighter than the sun. Gimle was special, for at the end of time, when both heaven and earth have passed away Gimle will still stand. Here righteous men and gods who had survived the fiery holocaust will dwell.

Connecting Asgard to Midgard, from Heaven to Earth was a sacred bridge, Bifrost, the 'Quivering Roadway'. This bridge was built of fire, water and air. It quivered and changed colours, looking like a rainbow. The Edda described it:

"Have you been told that the gods built a bridge from earth to heaven called Bifrost? You have seen it (but) maybe you call it the rainbow. It has three colours and is very strong, and made with more skill and cunning than other structures."[63]

It was on this bridge that the gods travelled to and fro from the Earth to the lands of the Otherworld. So when you next see a rainbow in the sky, pause and think that this was the ancient link for the Norse between one world and the next.

---

[63] The Prose Edda of Snorri Sturluson, Young, 1964:40.

NORSE COSMOLOGY
AND THE LANDS OF DEATH

The Norse had a very elaborate and intricate cosmology. There were nine distinct worlds, arranged in three levels. The figure of nine recurs again and again in Norse mythology. It was a mystical number of great symbolic significance. Heimdall, the guardian of the gods, had nine mothers. Odin's son Hermod, travels for nine nights to reclaim the god Baldur from the land of Hel. There are many other examples of the figure nine in Norse myth.

Nine is often a magical number in many religions. The ancient Egyptians called nine *'the Mountain of the Sun'*. To the classical Greeks nine was special. There were the Nine Muses who were conceived after nine nights of Zeus' lovemaking. Demeter spent nine days searching for her lost daughter Persephone. The gods were banished from their home, Olympus for nine full years for the crime of perjury.

Nine is the last of the single digits. As such it symbolises death and rebirth, the beginning and the end of a cycle.

Back to the world of the Norse. On the top level were: Alfheim, Land of the Light Elves; Vanaheim, Land of the Vanir; and in the utmost splendour and glory, Asgard, World of the Aesir, Home of the gods. In Asgard there was Valhalla, the Hall of the Slain, where the dead warriors lived.

In the middle level was: Midgard, Home of Man; Nidavellir, Land of the Dwarves; and Svartalfheim, Land of the Dark Elves. Svartalfheim was an underground world where these elves and dwarves lived in caves and potholes. In this level was also Jotunheim, Land of the Giants. In Jotunheim there was the giants' stronghold called Utgard, ruled by the evil giant Utgard-Loki.

The lowest level consisted of: Niflheim, the Land of the Dead. This was nine days ride northwards and downward from Midgard, the land of man. In Niflheim there was the realm of Hel, where evil men went to die. There was as well Muspell the land of Fire but we do not know on which level this world existed.

Figure 10 - Svartalfheim

All three levels were linked to the root of the great tree Yggdrasil, the Guardian Tree. This majestic ash tree had a root to all worlds. Snorri in the *Edda* describes it as: *"its branches spread out over the whole world and reach up over heaven."*[64]

We have looked at most of those worlds earlier. But perhaps it is worth looking a little deeper into the realms of death, Valhalla and Hel.

To take Valhalla first: this was a massive hall that housed the Einherjar, those dead heroic warriors awaiting the fall the world, Ragnarok. Here is the *Edda's* description of this vast palace:

> *"I think there are in Valhalla*
> *more than six hundred*
> *and forty doors;*
> *out of a single door at a time*
> *will tramp nine hundred and sixty men,*
> *champions advancing on the monster."*[65]

That is a great many warriors, nine hundred and sixty men from each of six hundred and forty doors. That is 614,400 men advancing at a time. It is also a massive amount of men to be housed in a single building.

It was also a very impressive looking palace. It was a high building; the hall was so tall that you could scarcely see above it. The walls were made from glistening spears, so highly polished that they illuminated the hall. Its roof was also special; it was made from highly polished golden shields. Over the gate at the entrance to the hall were a mystical boar's head and an eagle. These animals could see to the far corners of the world. It must have been a magnificent palace, worthy of heroes.

To the Norse warfare was honourable. To die in battle was the best death for a warrior. He would be welcomed into Valhalla as a champion. Odin was their god of war. His attendants were called Valkyries. These were young beautiful women with flowing blond hair. They wore dazzling silver or gold helmets, blood red corselets, and were armed with spears and sparkling shields. Valkyries rode white steeds,

---

[64] The Prose Edda of Snorri Sturluson, Young, 1964:42.
[65] The Prose Edda of Snorri Sturluson, Young, 1964:65.

seated on these animals they were seen as clouds and rode high on sky above battlefields choosing the warriors brave enough to honour Valhalla. They would swoop and pluck the dead from the battle to send them to the revered Valhalla, a place for worthy champions. These Choosers of the Slain also snatched the dead warriors from the sinking longboats. It was a great honour to be chosen by a Valkyrie. These maidens also presided over the feasts at Valhalla, pouring out the heavenly mead in horns for the fallen fighters. Here is a Valkyrie Song which describes these rather unusual mystical women:

> "Slowly they moved to the billow side;
> And the forms, as they grew more clear,
> Seem'd each on a tall pale steed to ride,
> And a shadowy crest to rear,
> And to beckon with faint hand
> From the dark and rocky strand,
> And to point a gleaming spear.
>
> Then a stillness on his spirit fell,
> Before th' unearthly train;
> For he knew Valhalla's daughters well,
> The chooser of the slain!"[66]

These daughters of Valhalla could be very cruel and bloodthirsty. Although they looked very beautiful they were capable of very sadistic acts. They poured rain from drops of blood on the land. There is a description of them riding through the sky on a ship through a torrent of blood. In one particularly gory account they are seated on a battlefield weaving a tapestry from human intestines. For this work of art they used an arrow for a shuttle and men's heads were used as weights to weigh down end of the cords of the tapestry. That must have been a spectacular representation of an artist's skill.

---

[66] Valkriur Song by Mrs Hemans, in The Norsemen (Myths and Legends), Guerber, 1994:161.

Figure 11 - Valkyrie

Valhalla itself was a Viking warrior's paradise; there was ample drinking and fighting. In fact such was the fighting, that every day in the great courtyard, during daylight warriors could engage in battle maim and kill themselves. Sometimes terrible wounds would occur. But in the evening when the dinner horn sounded, they would arise whole and healthy again, being miraculously cured and all ready to continue the fray afresh.

There was abundant food in Valhalla. A magical boar called Seahrimnir, was boiled every day in a cauldron called Eldhrimnir, meaning *'Fire-sooty'*. Every evening this mystical beast came alive again, ensuring plenty of pork for all. The cook who prepared this magical feast was called Andhrimnir, *'Sooty-face'*. No one went hungry in Valhalla.

It was a similar tale with drink. There were abundant refreshments. A magical she goat called Heidrun dwelt there. From her ample teats ran mead, so much mead that a bottomless cauldron was filled every day with the refreshing liquid. A merry time was had by all.

Valhalla contained everything that a Northern warrior could wish for. You can see why in those far off days Odin and his revered place, Valhalla was so popular.

Now the realm of Hel: this was situated under the earth. It is a region of the icy cold Niflheim. Like Valhalla it a land of the dead. But whereas Valhalla welcomed heroes, Hel was the place for those who died from illness and old age. To die in such a manner was not a fitting death for a brave warrior, who should die in battle. To die of what we would in the modern day call natural causes, would be a cause of shame to a Viking. This was contemptuously called a *'straw death'*, a reference to the fact the Viking beds were normally made from straw. The wicked would also go to Hel and from there to Niflhel, the Abode of Darkness. Sins considered wicked to the Norse were the forswearing of oaths and murder.

The realm of Hel was reached by a harsh, oppressive and painful journey. The road to Hel started in a grim black cave called Gnipahellir, set among towering cliffs. This cave was guarded by the chained hound of Hel, a fearsome beast called Garm. Garm has a blood spattered coat, presumably from the men that he has eaten. Garm will only become free at the end of the world, Ragnarok, for then the way to Hel will be open.

This image of the Hound of Hell is interesting and appears in other ancient religions. The Greeks had a monstrous many headed dog called Cerberus who guarded the entrance to Hades, the Greek Underworld, the world of the dead. This animal was said to have many heads, the figure varying from three to a hundred in different tales. A truly hideous beast he had a dragons tail and a mane of serpents heads; a demon of Hell.

The road to Hel was so harsh that it took Hermod, who tried to recover the god Baldur from Hel, nine hard days to reach. In the *Edda* his journey is described: *"he rode dales so deep and dark that he saw nothing, until he reached the river Gjoll."* This river marked the boundary to Hel from Niflheim. Again the *Edda* gives a description of the route to this dreadful place; *"the road to Hel lies downwards and northwards."*

The River Gjoll, meaning *'Howling'* or *'Echoing'*, a very graphic name giving a vivid picture of this formidable boundary to the realm of Hel. This stretch of water was crossed by a bridge. This bridge had a thatch of gleaming gold and was guarded by a maiden called Modgud.

There is an alternative version of this story of the river that borders Hel. Here it is called Gioll. The bridge is still golden but instead of thatch it is now made from crystal. It is hung on a single hair. Modgud the guardian of the bridge is now a skeleton who makes every spirit pay a toll of blood before they can pass into Hel. Here is a graphic piece of poetry from the *'Valhalla'* describing the scene:

> *"The bridge of glass hung on a hair*
> *Thrown o`er the river terrible,-*
> *The Gioll, boundary of Hel.*
> *Now here the maiden Modgud stood,*
> *Waiting to take the toll of blood,-*
> *A maiden horrible to sight,*
> *Fleshless, with shroud and pall bedlight."*[67]

---

[67] The Norsemen (Myths and Legends), Guerber, 1994:181.

Figure 12 - Hel

A truly gruesome and ghastly sight. This was the bridge to Hel, here travelled the spirits to the eventual end of their journey. In a Viking funeral pile there was normally a horse or a wagon. The purpose of these was to carry the dead to their resting place. That seems a bit hard on the poor horse. In one grave in Oseberg there were found the bones of about thirteen horses. The Norse also bound on the bodies of the dead a strong pair of shoes before they were burnt on the pyre. This enabled them to complete their long journey over the long and hard roads without too much hardship.

Here we have more parallels with the classical Greek. Gjoll has a counterpart with the Greek River Styx, the chief river of Hades, the Greek Underworld. So important was the Styx to the Greeks, that there most binding oath was taken calling on the name of the Styx. If this oath was broken the person forsaking the oath would die within a year.

The warden of the bridge, Modgud, is similar to the ferryman Charon in Greek mythology. Charon rowed the spirits of the dead across the river Acheron in Hades. Acheron was the river of woe in the Underworld. Charon is represented in Greek legends as grey and ugly. He is clad in dirty garments and cap. Not quite so macabre as the skeleton of Modgud.

In the realm of Hel, was the goddess Hel, the goddess of death. She was the daughter of Loki, the god of evil and the giantess Angrboda, 'Boder-of-sorrow'. She was born in a dark cave in Jotunheim, the Land of the Giants. Loki and Angrboda also bore the terrible wolf Fenrir and the World Serpent, Jormungand.

Loki's children scared the gods; Jormungand was flung into the deep sea that surrounds the world. Here he grew into an enormous serpent, so vast that he encircled the whole of Midgard, the Land of Man. This creature lies on the sea bed, coiling around all mankind, with its tail in its mouth.

The wolf Fenrir was bound with a strong chain called Laeding, by the gods, but the wolf was too strong for them, Laeding snapped. The gods tried again with a stronger chain, Droma, but again the chain broke. It appeared that nothing could restrain Fenrir. The gods sent a messenger Skirnir, to the world of the dark elves, Svartalfheim, to ask for advice. A slender thread called Gleipnir was made. But would this be strong enough? It was made from six strange ingredients: the sound a cat makes when it moves; a woman's beard; the roots of a mountain; the sinews of a bear; the breath of a fish; and a bird's spittle. But Gleipnir was magic, and this slight and skinny thread worked where the heavy chains had failed. Fenrir was bound, although his protesting screams were horrible to be heard. He will only be free at Ragnarok, the end of the world.

The goddess Hel was thrown into the cold world on Niflheim where she became the guardian of the land of Hel, where men went who had not died an honourable warriors death.

Hel, the serpent Jormungand, and the wolf Fenrir, became the symbols of pain, sin, and death, in the Viking world. Here is a section from *Valhalla* describing this monstrous trio:

> "Now Loki comes, cause of all ill!
> Men and Aesir (the gods) curse him still.
> Long shall the gods deplore,
> Even till Time be o'er,
> His base fraud on Asgard's hill.
> While, deep in Jotunheim, most fell,
> Are Fenrir, Serpent, and Dread Hel,
> Pain, Sin, and Death, his children three,
> Brought up and cherished; thro' them he
> Tormentor of the world shall be."[68]

Hel lived in a homestead called Elvidnir, meaning *'Damp with sleet'*. There is a rather bleak description of this Hall in the *Edda*. It had high walls and huge gates. Inside, she has a plate called *'Hunger'*. Her knife was *'Famine'*. She had two servants, a man called Ganglati, *'Slow moving'*, and a maid called Ganglot, also *'Slow moving'*. The stone at the entrance was called *'Drop to destruction'*. She also had a bed called *'Sick bed'* surrounded by hangings called *'Glimmering Misfortune'*. Here is a graphic description of Hel's hall, Evidner, in the *Valhalla*:

---

[68] The Norsemen (Myths and Legends), Guerber, 1994:179.

Figure 13 - Loki's Children

"Elvidner was Hela's hall,
Iron-barred, with massive wall;
Horrible that palace tall!
Hunger was her table bare;
Waste, her knife; her bed, sharp Care;
Burning Anguish spread her feast;
Bleached bones arrayed each guest;
Plague and Famine sang their runes,
Mingled with Despair's harsh tunes.
Misery and Agony
E'er in Hel's abode shall be!"[69]

Hel herself was quite distinctive, she was half black, and half flesh coloured, giving her the appearance of looking grim and gloomy. In time of plague or famine she would don a three legged horse and rake up those who escaped death by illness. During the virulent epidemics of the Black Death Hel was said to have used a broom in collecting fallen souls.

Those were cruel times. Life was hard, and for those not dying a warrior's death it would become harder still.

---

[69] Ibid, 1994:179.

RAGNAROK
THE NORSE END OF THE WORLD

In Northern mythology as well as having a creation myth they also had a legend about the end of the world. This was called Ragnarok, meaning *'The Twilight of the Gods'*. In the Christian religion the end of the world is forecast by the Armageddon, in *Revelations* in the *New Testament*. This is when there will be a vast battle between the forces of good and evil in the last days of the world. Similarly in Ragnarok there will be a final battle in which the gods will surrender to the forces of evil. Although in *Revelations* good will win, in Ragnarok the gods will lose and all creation be destroyed.

Ragnarok will start with a dreadful winter called the Fimbulvetr, literally meaning *'terrible winter'*. This will last for three winters with no break for summer in-between. There will be snowy blizzards from all the four quarters of the earth. The wind will howl and there will be razor sharp frosts. The weather will be appallingly cold with no sun at all.

For three years up to Fimbulvetr there will be constant warfare in the world. Greed will be paramount. Brother will kill brother. There will be incest, mothers seducing their sons and fathers their daughters. There will be great bloodshed for no reason. Chaos will rule. This is described in the *Poetic Edda*:

> *"Brother will fight*
> *and kill each other,*
> *siblings*
> *do incest;*
> *men will*
> *know misery,*
> *adulteries be multiplied,*
> *an axe-age, a sword-age,*
> *shields will be cloven,*
> *a wind-age, a wolf-age,*
> *before the world's ruin."*[70]

---

[70] The Poetic Edda, Dronke (trans), 1969:19

Figure 14 - Ragnarok

It will be a time of catastrophe. The end of the world will be disastrous. Blood will flow and unhappiness prevalent.

There is a theory suggested by the Danish anthropologist Olrik. He has traced many similarities between the Icelandic and Persian myths. Here there is a cataclysmic winter, harsh in its severity, very similar to the Fimbulvetr winter of Ragnarok. This winter would last for three years, as did Fimbulvetr. Yima the Persian god of death builds a 'vara', an underground retreat. This shelters men, women, cattle and plants so that after the holocaust mankind can rebuild and there can be life anew. But it must be said that birth and rebirth are common religious symbols.

Now the end of the world will start. Sol and Mani the sun and the moon in their radiant heavenly driven chariots frantically look back. The demon wolves called Skoll and Hati were gaining on them. Skoll caught the sun and obliterated her in his fierce jaws. Mankind was doomed. His brother Hati captured the moon and crushed it in his ferocious jaws. The demonic wolves had blood dripping from their mouths. The stars disappeared from heaven. Light was obliterated from the earth and the world was plunged into darkness.

The earth itself will tremble. Trees will be uprooted. The whole world shakes. Now the wolf Fenrir is loose, he has escaped from his chains. This is a monstrous beast. His eyes and nostrils blaze with fire. A mammoth creature, Fenrir advances with his mouth open, the upper jaw stretching far against the sky, his lower jaw touching the earth. This fiendish brute advanced over the earth blazing flames from his nostril and eyes; a truly revolting and repulsive sight.

More monsters appeared, each as terrifying as the other. Due to the vast shaking of the earth, the sea will lash over the lands. There will be massive floods. Tidal waves will rise higher and higher engulfing everything. The Midgard serpent is writhing in fury trying to get free. This fearful serpent will buckle and writhe out of the sea and rise on to land. She will blow clouds of poison, spattering the sky and the sea. Water will be contaminated. Here is a description of the effects of this horrendous beast from the *Valhalla*:

> "In giant wrath the Serpent tossed
> In ocean depths, till, free from chain,
> He rose upon the foaming main;
> Beneath the lashings of his tail,
> Seas, mountain high, swelled on the land;
> Then, darting mad the waves acrost,

Pouring forth bloody froth like hail,
Spurting with poisoned, venomed breath
Foul, deadly mists o'er all the Earth,
Thro' thundering surge, he sought the strand."[71]

Now the ship Naglfar is released. This ship is entirely made from dead men's nails. For it was the custom for the deceased's family to cut the nails of the dead. If this was not done the nails would go to build this fearsome vessel and the end of the world would become that bit nearer. This terrifying ship would be steered by a giant called Hrym.

Now come the giants from Muspell. They are led by blazing flame giant Surt, he is surrounded by flames, his sword shining brighter than the sun. They gallop over Bifrost, the rainbow bridge that links the world of man, Midgard to Asgard, the world of the gods. The bridge weakened by the weight of the fire giants now collapses. Here is the terrifying description of those dreadful days in *Valhalla*:

"Down thro' the fields o fair,
With glittering armour fair,
In battle order bright,
They sped while seething flame
From rapid hoofstrokes came.
Leading his gleaming band, rode Surtur (Surt),
`Mid the red ranks of raging fire."[72]

The fire giants continue until they reach the plain of Vigrid. Vigrid is a huge plain a hundred and twenty leagues wide and one hundred and twenty leagues long. It needs to be a vast area in which this final battle will be fought. It is difficult to know how long a league was, an English league was three statute miles (4.8km), although it varies in different countries. Vigrid is on Asgard and appears to be similar to Armageddon, the place where the last battle shall be fought. Here they meet the monstrous Fenrir the wolf and the ferocious Midgard Serpent. But there are other ogres waiting here for the last battle to commence. Here is the mischief making Loki, the trickster god. He is with the giant Hrym. All the frost giants gather to do battle as do the family of Hel, goddess of Death, who arises from beneath the earth. The hound of Hel, Garm, breaks free from his chains and

---

[71] The Norsemen (Myths and Legends), Guerber, 1994:332.
[72] The Norsemen (Myths and Legends), Guerber, 1994:333.

leaps from his home eager to join the final conflict. Now the dragon Nidhogg who eats the corpses of evil doers flies over the battlefield with corpses on his wings. In this final confrontation all the giants from the land of fire Muspell, amass to form a blazing army. The final stage is set. The end is near.

Now Heimdall watchman of the gods and guardian of the rainbow bridge blows on Gjoll, his sacred horn, signalling the end of the world. Such a blast will be blown on the instrument that all gods and men will hear throughout the whole nine worlds of the Norse cosmos. Long trumpet horns have been found by archaeologists in Danish peat bogs. They date from the Late Bronze Age and are a very old musical instrument called a lur. This was a long bronze horn which had a double curve and a disc-shaped mouth. They look a bit like a snake. They were usually found in pairs. On a cauldron found at Gundestrup, Jutland, Denmark, is depicted very long straight lurs being played with bronze animal heads on the top of the horns, acting as the bell of the instrument.

Trumpet horns were used by the ancient Irish Celts in battle. Noise definitely played a large part ancient warfare and the strident sound of those old braying war trumpets would have played their part. The sound must have scared the enemy, who would have heard it from a great distance, striking fear into its heart.

John Purser wrote at length on the war trumpet known as the Deskford Carnyx. Although talking about Irish horns, he gives an idea of what sound would have come from such an instrument:

> "There is no question that the instrument was used in battle. On coins it is shown in the hands of mounted warriors at full gallop (arguing for the great integral strength in the design of the instrument),in association with shields and Gaulish warriors. It is capable of producing a sound of immense power. It can be as loud as a modern trombone, the most powerful instrument in the symphony orchestra. What is more the manner in which it is held means that the sound travels unimpeded from the instrument well over the heads of the surrounding armies and could have been used to terrify the opposition, encourage the lads, or to convey signals. Indeed, we could imagine a sneaky Proto-Pict making his way at night to the bottom of the Antonine Wall, raising the head of the Carnyx over the

wooden palisade which surmounted it, and scaring the Roman sentries into involuntary bowel evacuation with a few fearsome blasts, before disappearing into the mists......"[73]

Trumpets have a religious significance in many religions. Angels are depicted blowing long trumpets. In the *Old Testament* of the bible the walls of Jericho were brought down by the sound of trumpets. There is a parallel with Christianity and the Norse religion in that trumpets blasted to herald the last Judgement in the *New Testament* of the Bible, as it did the end of the world to the Norse, Ragnarok.

In the Greek religion too trumpets played a part. The Athene Salinx, the trumpet player from Argos who carried the trumpet that joined Heaven and Earth in common rejoicing. One of the functions of the Greek goddess Athena was as a war goddess and protector of cities. The Greeks also used trumpets in their rituals. In the Dionysian festival held at Lerna, Dionysus, god of wine, was evoked from the marshes by the blowing of trumpets.

The trumpet was also important to the Romans. In fact, they held a special ceremony twice a year to purify these instruments. This was called Tubilustrium and was held on the 23rd of March and repeated on the 23rd May. It was one of Rome's many ceremonies to honour the Roman army.

There is appears to be a connection between trumpets, battle and religion. Armies always went into battle in the name of the gods of their own belief system. At the start of the combat the trumpet would be blown, the battle charge, signifying the sacred nature of warfare. Even in modern times in the army important periods of the day such as reveille, are proclaimed by the blowing of a horn. You still sound the charge at the start of a battle.

Traditionally trumpets symbolises an important climaxing of elements and events marked by celestial manifestation. This is personified in air, breath and sound which are used to make the instruments unique noise.

The gods now realise the Ragnarok is here, the final conflict has come. They meet to plan a course of action. Odin rides to ask the wise Mimir for advice. Mimir's head guarded a well, known as Mimir's Well, at the base of the sacred tree Yggdrasil. His head was a valuable source of knowledge which Odin used at times of crisis.

---

[73] Scotland's Music, Purser, 1993

It is a time of terror. Even the sacred tree Yggdrasil trembles in fear. There will be the sound of cocks crowing in the air. The red cock Fjalar will crow over Valhalla, the land of fallen heroes, this will be echoed the golden combed Gullinkambi crowing to the gods and mankind in Midgard. The dead will be raised in the dark realms of Hel by the sound of a rust red cock. The cock's cries will warn that the devastation is here, take heed.

Now all the Aesir, the gods and the Einherjar, those heroic dead warriors waiting in Valhalla, will rise and don armour to fight for the preservation of the world. The Einherjar represent a massive fighting force of the bravest soldiers. From their home Valhalla pours out eight hundred armed men through each of five hundred and forty doors, a truly massive army struggling to save the world.

This fearsome army will be led by the great god Odin, the All-Father. Odin will be resplendent in a magnificent gold helmet and a superb coat of mail, looking every inch a worthy opponent to the forces of evil amassed around him. He will carry his magical spear Gungnir, specially made for him by the dwarves, those master craftsmen of steel. The gods prepare for battle. But after many previous adventures the gods were now weakened. Odin had only one eye, Tyr but one hand, and Freyr no longer had his sword, only a stag's horn, to defend himself with. But still they bravely assembled and rode to the battlefield to fight the demons of evil and save the world.

Opposing the gods and the Einherjar were the monsters of evil. Similar to Armageddon it was a battle of good over evil. Facing the gods were the fire giant Surt, billowing flames, the army of the frost giants, the army of the goddess Hel, with her ferocious Hound of Hel Garm. There were also Loki, the trickster god and his monstrous children, Fenrir, a giant wolf blazing with fire, and the Midgard Serpent also a creature breathing fire and belching poisonous vapours. A truly terrifying collection of monsters, enough to make ones blood run cold. The final battle was to begin.

The battle begins. Odin locks in deadly combat with the fiend wolf, Fenrir. Fenrir massive jaws open wide, filling the space between heaven and earth and swallow Odin. It is in this strange manner that the father of the gods, Odin dies, one of the first of the gods to be slain. Here the large open mouth of the wolf symbolises, a cavern, the Underworld, darkness. So you have light being devoured by darkness. There is a similar event in the Vedic *Rig Veda*. Here the wolf devours the quail, another symbol of light. This theme is common in folklore. In the story of Little Red Riding Hood there is a wolf that eats people.

But now his son Vidor born from Odin and the giantess Grid, goes to avenge his father's death and attacks the evil Fenrir. He puts his foot on the lower jaw of the enormous wolf. He has on special shoes. These shoes are made from strips of leather which men had pared off the toes and heels of their shoes. These were donated to the gods by man in preparation of this day. Many of these thin strips had to be collected for Vidor to protect his feet from the vicious Fenrir's mouth. But now they came in to their own. Vidor was able to step into the jaws of the giant beast. With his feet holding the lower jaw down he wretched open the animal's upper jaw and tore open his throat. This terrifying beast was now dead.

Thor is attacked by the Midgard Serpent. The serpent blows vile poison all over him. Thor battles on bravely and manages to slay the creature. But his victory is short lived. He staggers back nine paces, finally overcome by the flood of venom from the dying monster. Another god is dead.

Freyr, a fertility god, is assaulted by the fire giant Surt. The god had unfortunately given his sword to his servant Skinir, thus sealing his own death warrant. He is now unarmed against the Surt's flaming blade. But he fights on bravely, although he cannot compete with the monster. Freyr dies in this last confrontation.

Tyr, the god of war and one of the bravest of gods battles with the demon hound, Garm, now freed from his chains and the confines of his cave in Hel. It is a bitter struggle. Neither wins, for they end up killing each other.

The same thing happens in the fight between Loki, the trickster god and his arch enemy Heimdall, the messenger of the gods and the guardian of the Rainbow Bridge. For these two also end up slaying each other.

The gods are now dead as are the brave warriors from Valhalla, the Einherjar. All mankind has died. The world as we know it comes to an end. Then fire giant Surt engulfs the world in flames. Heaven, Earth, all the nine worlds of the Norse cosmology is immersed in. Even Yggdrasil is burned down. Such is the heat that the seas will boil. The sun will darken and the stars disappear. All will be dark. The earth will vanish into the sea. There is a total holocaust. Here is the description of the dreadful catastrophe in the *Edda*:

> "The sun will go black
> earth sink in the sea,

heaven will be stripped
of its bright stars;
smoke rage
and fire,
leaping the flame
lick heaven itself."[74]

There are strong parallels between the Norse Ragnarok and the Christian Armageddon prophesied in the *New Testament* of the Bible. But it must be remembered that during this period it was feared that the world would end in either 1000 or 1033 CE. It was thought that Doomsday would occur at the coming millennium. This Christian concept could have been transferred in the writing down of the old Icelandic customs by the scribes.

Here is the Last Judgement being foretold in the *Gospel of Mark*:

> *"But in those days, after that tribulation, the sun shall be darkened, and the moon shall not give her light,*
> *And the stars of heaven shall fall, and the powers that are in heaven shall be shaken."*[75]

In Ragnarok the sun disappears and the stars darken, just as was prophesied in the bible. This gloomy forecast of the end of the world with *"the sun becoming as black as sackcloth of hair and the moon became as blood"* is repeated in *Revelation 6:12*. In 6:13 the *"stars of heaven fell unto the earth"* is again repeating the theme of darkness.

In *Revelations* there is a section in Chapter 8 where seven angels sound seven trumpets similar to the trumpet blast announcing the start of Ragnarok. Here verse 7 describing the effect of the first blast of the instrument:

> *"And the first angels sounded, and there followed hail and fire mingled with blood, and they were cast upon the earth: and the third part of trees was burnt up, and all green grass was burnt up."*[76]

As in Ragnarok there are similar themes of blood and fire and devastation. It is interesting the references to fire. In the Ragnarok there are the sons of Muspell, led by the fire giant Surt. Muspelle appears in a late ninth century

---

[74] The Prose Edda of Snorri Sturluson, Young, 1964:90.
[75] Mark 13:24-25.
[76] Revelation 8:7.

Bavarian poem. It is taken to mean the *"fire that will burn the world"*. There seems to be a strong connection between fire and the end of the world in both traditions.

But Ragnarok is not totally the end. The Norse believed in regeneration, new life and rebirth. A new world would be built on the smouldering ashes of the old one. Life will begin again.

The earth will rise up from the sea. The sun bears a daughter, a beautiful girl, born before the wolf devours her mother. She now shines over the earth. The land will be green again. Corn will grow in the fields that were never sown. Nature will be reborn.

Vidor, and Vali both sons of Odin, and Modi and Magni, the sons of Thor survive the holocaust. They will dwell in Idavoll a shiny plain where there once was Asgard, the home of the gods. They will be joined by Baldur and his twin brother Hod, back from the world of the dead. They will talk and reminisce over times past.

There will still be heaven. Here will be Gimle, where the surviving gods will find shelter; this has escaped the fire of Ragnarok. In Gimle there is a hall called Brimir in a land that is never cold called Okolnir. Brimir has endless supplies of drink, those staying there will be forever merry. It is the home of giants. On the dark mountains of Nidafjoll there is a hall called Sindri, this is a beautiful palace made of red gold. In these palaces will live the good and righteous.

But there will also be a Hel, called Nastrand, the *'Shore of Corpses'*. This was a dreadful place. There was a cold north facing hall. The walls and roof were made from writhing serpents, woven together like wattle, or basket work. The heads of these serpents faced into the house, spewing poisonous venom throughout the hall. There was so much venom that it flowed in toxic torrents. This description of this grim place is from the *Edda*:

> *"I know a hall*
> *whose doors face north*
> *on Nastrand*
> *far from the sun,*
> *poison drips*
> *from lights in the roof;*
> *that building is woven*
> *of back of snakes.*
> *There heavy streams*
> *must be waded through*
> *by breakers of pledges*

and murderers".[77]

If that was not enough, it was here that the dragon, Nidhogg, gnawed the bones of the dead, from the cauldron Hvergelmir. It was not a good idea to be a murderer or oath breaker in the days of the Vikings.

The image of snakes writhing in a hall bears a resemblance to that of snake pits. These were a fairly common form of torture in England during this period. According to the Norse poem *Krakumal*, the Viking Ragnor Lodbrok was thrown into a snake pit by King Ella, of Northumbria. With his dying breath Ragnor says: *"Goinn has housed himself in my heart!"* Goinn was the name of one of the serpents at the root of the sacred ash tree, Yggdrasil. It is difficult to date this story but King Ella died in 867 CE.

There was also a reference to snake-pits in the *Anglo-Saxon Chronicle* under items for the year 1137 CE. Those were harsh days; many different forms of torture were used. The passage describes some of them. It appears that the Anglo-Saxons could be as cruel as the Vikings. Here is the description from the Laud version of the *Chronicle* about the Saxons themselves:

> *"By night and by day they seized those whom they believed to have any wealth, whether they were men or women; and in order to get their gold and silver, they put them into prison and tortured them with unspeakable tortures, for never martyrs tortured as they were, They hung them up by the feet and smoked them with foul smoke. They strung them up by the thumbs, or by the head, and hung coats of mail on their feet. They tied knotted cords round their heads and twisted it till it entered the brain. They put them in dungeons wherein were adders and snakes and toads, and so destroyed them. Some they put into a 'crucethus'; that is to say, into a short, narrow, shallow chest into which they put sharp stones; and they crushed the man in it until they had broken every bone in his body. In many of the castles were certain instruments of torture so heavy that two or three men had enough to do to carry one. It was made in this way: a weight was fastened to a beam which was attached to a sharp iron put round the man's throat and neck so that he could move in no direction, and*

---

[77] The Prose Edda of Snorri Sturluson, Young, 1964:91.

could neither sit, nor lie, nor sleep, but had to bear the whole weight of the iron. Many thousands they starved to death."[78]

But not all men died in Ragnarok. Two people hide in Hoddmfmir's Wood, a woman called Lif and a man Lofthrasir. They survive on morning dew. Together these survivors rebuild mankind. A whole new race of men develops. The world starts anew.

But there are fragments of Icelandic verse that add an extra verse to the saga. In the *Hauksbok* manuscript there is this:

*"Then comes a ruler
to keep dominion,
a mighty lord
majestic over all..."*[79]

This theme is echoed in a late twelfth century manuscript *Voluspa bin Skamma*:

*"Then comes one
who is greater than all,
though never his name
do I dare to name;
few now see
in the future further
than the moment Odin
is to meet the Wolf."*[80]

These fragments of verse suggest Christian overtones were added to the original pagan sagas. They seem reminiscent of the Second Coming of Jesus Christ in Christian traditions. But a lot of old traditional observances were subsumed into the newer Christianity. Though the original concept of rebirth is an ancient one found in many old civilisations stretching back through thousands of years.

---

[78] The Anglo-Saxon Chronicle, Garmonsway (trans), 1975:264.
[79] Tolkien and the Invention of Myth: A Reader, Chance, 2004:184.
[80] Tolkien and the Invention of Myth: A Reader, Chance, 2004:185.

PART 4
THE NORSE GODS AND MYTHS
EXPRESSED THROUGH THE
DAYS OF THE WEEK

SUNDAY

Sunday is the first day of the week. The name comes from the Latin *dies solis*, meaning *'day of the sun'*. Originally this was meant to be a pagan sun god, but as Sunday developed into the Christian Sabbath, this was taken to mean God. Biblically God was described as *'Sun of righteousness'* very fitting for a day of worship and rest.

The sun was very important to ancient cultures. It was a source of heat and light and as such seen as divine. All the major religions had their own sun god. The Assyrians and Babylonians had Shamash. The Persian sun god was Mithras. The sun to the Egyptians was Ra, to the Greeks, Helios.

To most ancient cultures the sun was male, though to the Norse the sun was female, called Sol, meaning *'sun'*. Snorri in the *Edda* distinctly calls Sol a goddess, this is rare. According to Snorri the sun and the moon were the children of the giant Mundilfari. Here is the description from the *Edda*:

> *"There was a man called Mundilfari who had two children. They were so fair and beautiful that he called one of them Moon and the other a daughter, Sun; he married her to a man called Glen (the name translates as glow). The gods, however, were angered at his arrogance and took the brother and sister and put them up in the sky. They made Sun drive the horses which drew the chariot of the sun that the gods had made to light the worlds from a spark which flew from Muspell. The horses are called Arvak and Alsvid (meaning Early waker and All strong). Under the shoulder-blades of the horses the gods put two bellows to cool them, and in some poems that is called iron-cold (literally meaning iron coal)."*[81]

The reference to the goddess Sol, pulling a chariot is interesting. There appears to be a parallel here in other

---

[81] The Prose Edda of Snorri Sturluson, Young, 1964:38.

civilisations. The Greeks who called their sun god Helios, and he also drove a chariot through the sky. Helios would rise in his chariot from Oceanus in the east and surge through the sky descending in the evening into Oceanus in the west. His chariot would be pulled by four horses. The Roman equivalent, the sun god Sol, probably Sol Indiges, also drove a Roman quadriga, a chariot drawn by a team of four horses. In Rhodes, the ancient Greeks worshipped the sun as their chief deity, would annually dedicate a chariot and four horses to Helios and thrown both the chariot and the horses into the sea for the gods use.

This link to horses, chariots and the sun appears common. The kings of Judah dedicated chariots and horses to the sun. The Persians, Massagetae and the Spartans sacrificed horses to their sun god. The latter of these, the Spartans, made this sacrifice of the top of Mount Taygetus, a spectacular mountain range where they used to see the sun set every day.

The Persian god sun god, Mithra is often described as riding in a chariot pulled by white horses. As Mitra, Mithra is one of the oldest Aryan gods. His name means contract or covenant. So he became the god of mutual agreement. To sanctify a pact or contract a bull would be sacrificed to Mithra, to be followed by a sacrificial meal. The word *'mitra'* from this god came to mean *'friend'*. Even today in modern Iran the Persian word *'mihr'*, derived from *mithra*, means *'the sun'* and *'mutual love'*.

Mitra was also known as the sun god Surya. In this context he drives a chariot pulled by seven red mares. This is a Hindu sun god who was worshipped from 1700 BCE and is still worshipped today. He is the god not only of the sun but also of cosmic order and as such is a source of infinite knowledge. There are many statues of this sun god throughout India.

Archaeologically there is a representation of this theme of the sun being carried in a chariot found at Trundholm in a peat bog in Denmark. Here farmers found a bronze figure of a horse and part of a cart with a large bronze disc in it. The horse had a harness with star or sun decorating the eyes of the animal. The bronze disc was approx. 25cm or 10 inches in diameter. It was gilded on one side with a thin sheet of gold but the other side was left bronze. The cart had six wheels. The whole model was about 60cm or 24 inches long. It can be dated to about 1300 BCE.

The wagon was broken as was common in religious ceremonies in those days. Items were ritually broken before being offered to the gods. The model would have represented the sun. The gilded side of the orb represented the light and heat of the sun travelling around the sky. The bronze side represented the red sunset as the sun went underground on its journey to the Otherworld. The ceremony would have been a striking example of ritual to the sun god in those far off days.

The best known sun gods were those of the classical Romans, Apollo and his counterpart to the Greek, Helios. Here is a poetic description of the beautiful and powerful Roman god of the sun, Apollo by the poet Pike:

> "Bright-hair'd Apollo! - thou who ever art
> A blessing to the world - whose mighty heart
> Forever pours out love, and light, and life;
> Thou, at whose glance, all things of earth are rife
> With happiness; to whom, in early spring,
> Bright flowers raise up their heads, where'er they cling
> On the steep mountain side, or in the vale
> Are nestled calmly. Thou at whom the pale
> And weary earth looks up, when winter flees,
> With patent gaze: thou for whom wind-stripped trees
> Put on flesh leaves, and drink deep of the light
> That glitters in thine eye: thou in whose bright
> And hottest rays the eagle fills his eye
> With quenchless fire, and far, far up on high
> Screams out his joy to thee, by all the names
> That thou dost bear - whether thy godhead claims
> Phoebus or Sol, or golden-hair'd Apollo,
> Cynthian or Pythian, if thou dost follow
> The fleeing night, oh, hear
> Our hymn to thee, and willingly draw near!"[82]

The Norse equivalent of Apollo the Greek sun god is Baldur. His name means lord. Baldur is a radiant god of sunshine and the sun. He was known as Baldur the Good, the son the great Odin and Frigg.

---

[82] Greece and Rome (Myths & Legends), Guerber, 1994:43

Here is Snorri's description of Baldur:

> *"Another son of Odin's is called Baldur, and there is (nothing but) good to be told of him. He is the best of them and everyone sings his praises. He is fair of face and bright that a splendour radiates from him, and there is one flower so white that it is likened to Baldur's brow; it is the whitest of all flowers; From that you can tell how beautiful his body is, how bright his hair. He is the wisest of the gods, and sweetest spoken, and the most merciful, but it is a characteristic of his that once he has pronounced a judgement it can never be altered."*[83]

Baldur had his own hall in Asgard called Breidablik. This palace had a silver roof and golden pillars. Nothing impure could live in this hall.

Baldur had been having nightmares. He confided in Odin and Frigg. The Aesir decided that Baldur was in danger and needed protection. The goddess Frigg, the wife of Odin, and mother of Baldur, exacted an oath from fire and water, iron and all kinds of metals, stones, earth, trees, ailments, beasts, birds, poison and serpents. All these swore not to harm Baldur. Frigg was satisfied, Baldur was safe, and nothing could harm him. But one thing did not vow not to injure the god. The mistletoe, a parasite escaped the pledge. It was too young and weak. The plant was thought harmless.

All the gods were playing games with Baldur. They were throwing things at him. Stones and missiles, nothing harmed him. Baldur just smiled challenging the gods to continue. There was joy and mirth. Everyone was laughing.

Loki got jealous. He changed into the form of an old woman and visited Frigg. He asked the goddess what was the cause of the gods' hilarity. Frigg smiled and said that Baldur would not be injured as she had made a pact with all weapons and trees that none would damage him. But she also informed the disguised Loki that the she had omitted the mistletoe, thinking it of no consequence.

Loki had heard what he needed. He found the mistletoe and took it to the assembly of gods. Here he saw Hodur, Baldur's blind brother. Hodur was sad he had no sight and no missile so he could not join in the sport with the others.

---

[83] The Prose Edda of Snorri Sturluson, Young, 1964:51.

Loki said he would help. He led the blind god to the best spot to stand and guided him to the target. He placed the mistletoe in his hand telling the sightless god that it was just a twig. Hodur threw his dart. There were cries of horror from the others, Baldur had been hit, the mistletoe went right through him, and he fell to the ground dead.

Loki had tricked Hodur into killing his brother. The gods were appalled. There was weeping and lamentations. It was the greatest tragedy to befall the gods.

The inconsolable Frigg offered a reward to anyone that would bring her son back from the dead. There was a long hard road into the kingdom of Hel, but this had to be done to retrieve Baldur. Frigg would offer the goddess of death, Hel, a reward to release her son. Hermod the Bold answered her plea. Taking Odin's horse Sleipnir, he galloped away on his difficult journey.

Meanwhile the gods prepared Baldur's funeral. His dragon ship, Ringhorn, meaning Curved prow, would be used with a funeral pyre built on it. Baldur's ship was huge but all the weight of the gods could not launch it and the pyre had to be built while the boat was afloat. The gods asked for help from Giantland. An Ogress called Hyrrokkin arrived riding a wolf. The reins of the wolf were vipers. So ferocious was the wolf that it took four berserker warriors had to hold him. Hyrrokkin was strong, one shove and the boat slipped into the water. But such was the force of this push that the rollers on which the ship ran caught fire. The world trembled. Thor became angry and would have attacked the giantess but the other gods calmed him down. The boat was now launched, the funeral could continue.

Poor Nanna, Baldur's wife, collapsed and died from the intense grief that she felt from her husband's death. Her body was placed on the pyre so she could join her beloved spouse.

The pyre was elaborate. It was decorated with tapestry hangings and flowers. Weapons were placed on it. Baldur's horse complete with harness was laid on the pyre. Thorns, the symbol of sleep were also laid on the pyre. Odin, overcome with grief placed his mystical ring Draupnir on his son's funeral pyre. It was now set alight.

Thor raised his hammer, to bless the event. But a further tragedy happened. A dwarf called Lit ran in front of Thor, he was kicked into the flames and died.

Figure 15 - Baldur's Brow

The ship now drifted to sea. The flames glowed. Baldur's body was reduced to ashes. The ship let up the sky and the god went on his journey to the Otherworld of death. All the gods saw him go and came to pay their last respects. There was mourning throughout the land.

But Hermod was on his quest to recover Baldur from Hel. He travelled for nine nights and the journey was hard he had to cover a lot of harsh terrain. Finally he reached the river Gjoll on the borders of Hel. Here there was a bridge, but it was guarded by a woman called Modgud. Modgud said that the previous days five whole troops of men had ridden over the bridge, but he a single person had made a louder noise. He obviously was not dead. Why, she asked would a living person want to go to the land of the dead? Hermod answered that he was there to see Baldur and take him back to the land of the living. Modgud said: *"the road to Hel lies downwards and northwards."*

Hermod continued his journey and arrived at the massive and forbidding gates of Hel. He spurred his steed Hleipnir. The horse and rider cleared the gates and entered the land of Hel.

Hermod came to Eljudnir, Hel's banqueting hall. Here he saw Baldur and Nanna. But there were conditions to the release of Baldur. The goddess of death Hel did not believe that Baldur was that popular and that there was that much grief in his absence. She said: *"If everything in the world, both dead and alive, weeps for him, then he shall go back to the Aesir, but he shall remain with Hel if anyone objects or will not weep"*[84]

Hermod rode back to Asgard. He took with him the ring Draupnir which Baldur had returned to Odin. But he did not have Baldur and Nanna with him. Baldur was not released and Nanna refused to leave without her husband. She did though give Hermod gifts to take back to Asgard. For Frigg she gave some rich linen for a head-dress and a gold ring for Fulla.

Messengers were sent to the whole of the nine worlds. All of nature shed tears and cried for the return of Baldur. Only

---

[84] The Prose Edda of Snorri Sturluson, Young, 1964:53.

one person did not weep. This was a giantess sitting in a cave, called Thokk. She answered:

> *"Thokk will weep*
> *dry tears*
> *at Baldur's embarkation;*
> *the old fellow*
> *was no use to me*
> *alive or dead,*
> *let Hel hold what she has."*[85]

Sadly the messenger returned to Asgard. All had cried apart from one, but that was enough to keep the god stuck in Hel. But it was not Thokk who had kept Baldur incarcerated in the land of the dead, it was Loki. For Thokk was the trickster god Loki in disguise. Loki had now condemned Baldur to death twice.

But Baldur does come back. He is resurrected and returns to earth with Hodur from the land of Hel after the Ragnarok, the end of the world, one of the few survivors of the holocaust. Here is Snorri describing who will survive and what the earth will then be like:

> *"At that time earth will rise out of the sea and be green and fair, and fields of corn will grow that were never sown. Vidor and Vali will be living, so neither the sea or Surt's fire will have done them injury, and they will inhabit Idavoll where Asgard used to be. And the sons of Thor, Modi, and Magni, will come there and posses Mjollnir. After that Baldur and Hodur will come from Hel."*[86]

But Baldur's death had to be avenged. His father Odin courted Rind, the goddess of the frozen earth. The result of this union is Vali the Avenger. Vali grew up fast. On the day of his birth he entered Asgard. He slew Hodur with an arrow. Justice had been done, vengeance taken.

The story of the death of Baldur is full of symbolism. Baldur is the sun and light, the blind Hodur represents darkness. So the darkness of winter is victorious over the light of summer. Vali brings revenge and the coming of new light after the winter darkness. In the north there are long

---

[85] The Prose Edda of Snorri Sturluson, Young, 1964:53.
[86] The Prose Edda of Snorri Sturluson, Young, 1964:92.

winters and short summers. But even after the longest winter there is life anew in another summer.

There is Loki who as the god of fire is jealous of the light of the sun, Baldur. All the tears and crying symbolises the season of the spring and the thaw of winter. The sun, Baldur and vegetation, Nanna, send to heaven, Odin and Earth, Frigg the ring Draupnir, the symbol of fertility. Yet again another sign of life, birth and renewal.

There is also the general symbolism of Baldur and Hodur as the conflicting forces of good and evil. Loki represents the tempter, a demon figure.

There are many similarities with the legend of Baldur and that of the classical Greek Adonis. The goddess of love Aphrodite, had an intense love for the attractive and beautiful Adonis, an agricultural and fertility god. Adonis was killed by a wild boar while hunting. From his blood which dripped into the earth there sprung the flower, red anemone. The custom of women who worshipped Adonis giving an offering of flowers which symbolised their private parts came from this. In some shrines these women actually offered themselves sexually to strangers as a devotion to Adonis. Aphrodite was distraught with grief. She begged Zeus to intercede and let her join her lover in the underworld or let him return to the upper world. But Hades refused to let him go. A compromise was reached Adonis was allowed to spend half the year, the spring and summer on earth, but had to return to Hades for the rest of the year, the autumn and winter. The story was symbolic of fertility and death and rebirth.

The resemblance between the story of Adonis and that of Baldur are many. Both the names Adonis and Baldur mean 'lord'. Both gods are exceptionally handsome and very good looking. Both are intensely loved by a goddess, Baldur, by Nanna and Adonis by Aphrodite. Both goddesses are greatly distressed and grieve deeply for their loss of their loved one. Both gods die from a deep blood wound. They both descend from death into the Underworld, Baldur goes down to Hel, Adonis to Hades. There is a refusal in both stories by the deity responsible for the land of death, for the gods to return. In Baldur's case it is the goddess Hel and in Adonis' the god Hades. Both Baldur and Adonis are finally resurrected.

There is an old Christian poem written in Old English called *Dream of the Rood*. This was found carved in runes of the Ruthwell Cross in Dumfriesshire. It dates from the late seventh or early eighth centuries. The poem is about Christ dying on the cross and the story bears a striking resemblance to that of Baldur.

Baldur was attacked by missiles. The poem says: *"I was all wounded with arrows;"*[87]

Then there is the reference to a shining god. Baldur was god of light. A reference to weeping, also prominent in the Baldur story, which is strange as crying was not usually a feature of Norse myths or the Norse way of life at all. Here is the excerpt:

> *"Darkness had enveloped in clouds the corpse of the Lord, the shining splendour. The shadow came forth, dark beneath the clouds; all creation wept, lamented the death of the King; Christ was on the Cross."*[88]

Both Baldur and Christ died and were resurrected. Baldur was the god of light. When the Norse were first converted to Christianity, Christ was called the White Christ or *Hvita-Kristr*. There are certainly strong resemblances between the two mythologies.

---

[87] Anglo-Saxon Spirituality: Selected Writings, Boenig, 2001:261.
[88] Ibid, 2001:261.

MONDAY

Monday, the second day of the week, was called *Dies Lunae* by the Romans meaning the Moon's Day. In Old English this was Monandaeg. In most ancient civilisations the moon was considered female but to the Germanic and Norse nations it was a male deity. The moon was considered very powerful, if it was female and a goddess, that power would be their wives and men the warriors would be subservient to their wives.

There is a tradition of Monday being known as Saint Monday. Monday was said to be a non working day after the weekend. Colloquially it became a holiday or *'holy day'* of St. Monday. Benjamin Franklin, the American president told in his autobiography of how he gained the good will of his employer by never making a Saint Monday.

There is a lovely story concerning Monday. During the Civil War days Cromwell was encamped at Perth. One of his most zealous supporters died, a man called Monday. Cromwell offered a reward for the best piece of poetry summarising his death. A shoemaker from the town of Perth won the competition with the following verse:

> *"Blessed be the Sabbath Day.*
> *And cursed by worldly pelf,*
> *Tuesday will begin the week,*
> *Since Monday's hanged himself."*[89]

Cromwell was so pleased with the resultant poem that he decreed Monday to be a holiday for shoemakers. After that Monday became known as Cobblers Monday. In some parts of Yorkshire days devoted to inactivity and laziness are called Cobblers Mondays.

Most moon goddess were female, but the Norse deity attributed to the moon was male, Mani. Mani was the brother of Sol the sun goddess. Mani had a chariot which

---

[89] The Wordsworth Dictionary of Phrase and Fable, Evans, 1993:953

rode round the heavens pursued by wolves who eventually catch the moon at Ragnarok, the end of time. Here is Snorri's description of the moon:

> "Moon (Mani) governs the journeying of the moon and decides the time of its waxing and waning. He took from earth two children, known as Bil and Hjuki, as they were coming away from the spring called Byrgir carrying on their shoulders the pail called Soeg and the pole Simul. Their father's name is Vidfinn. These children accompany Moon, as may be seen from earth."[90]

This portion of the *Edda* is an early origin of the famous nursery rhyme of Jack and Jill, with Jack and Jill being Bil and Hjuki. As in the old rhyme they went up the hill to fetch a pail of water. Here instead of a hill, there is the moon, but they are still carrying their pail of water.

The man on the moon is Vidfinn. There is an old tradition that states that the man on the moon is carrying a bundle of thorns on his back. This is a punishment for gathering sticks on the Sabbath. This is a biblical story related in *Numbers 15:32-36*. Some say that this was Cain, the thorns symbolic of his sin in killing his brother. There is also a mythological tradition that says that the man in the moon is Endymion, the lover of the moon goddess.

There are parallels between the Norse moon god Mani and the Hindu moon god Soma. Both are male which is rare for a deity of the moon. Soma, like Mani drives a chariot through the sky. It is a special chariot, having three wheels and is drawn by ten horses as white as jasmine flowers. Soma's symbol is a silver crescent as befits a moon deity. The Hindu word for Monday, Somavara is named after Soma.

Soma married the 27 daughters of the Rishi Dasha. The Rishi were priests, poets and sages. Rishi Dasha was one of the original 14 Rishis who were born from the brain of Brahma. These were very spiritual people and portions of the Vedic hymns were revealed to them and then to the rest of the world. They were also the first men to be honoured with the power to perform valid sacrifices for the gods. The fact

---

[90] The Prose Edda of Snorri Sturluson, Young, 1964:38.

that there were 27 of these women is symbolic. There are 27 days of the sidereal orbit of the moon.

To the Hindus it is very auspicious to be born at the full moon. Such a person will be blessed with good fortune. The priests utter a special prayer:

> *"Oh Moon which hast no enemy! Son of the Sun-disk! Thou who advancest knowledge among men, who givest us protection from danger, who givest us power to overcome our enemies. May this prayer be efficacious!"*[91]

The Hindus have a sacred drink named Soma, it is a yellow fluid. This is the drink that makes the gods immortal and as such it is the most precious liquid in the universe. This yellow fluid is symbolic of the rays of the sun and the moon and the pouring rain. Therefore Soma is also called the Lord or King of streams and the bestower of fertility. The drink has the power of the god Soma, to make the blind see and the lame walk. The drink has great curative powers. It is also strength giving, the priests who drink Soma can slay at a glance. Soma is made by the process of the pressed plant which is strained through a woollen filter into vats containing milk and water. A yellow liquid is obtained in this manner.

There is the same drink in the Persian Zoroastrian faith. It is now called Haoma. The plant is described as green with pliant shoots, which are fleshy and fragrant. The plant that the Zoroastrians use is from the genus *Ephedra*. To make the drink the stems of the plant were pounded with a mortar and the resulting juice consecrated. The liquid was hallucinogenic and gave religious insight to the priests drinking it. It was considered to give the imbiber supernatural powers.

Here is a hymn for the preparation of the Haoma offering, from the Zoroastrian *Yasha 9*:

> *"Reverence to Haoma, good is Haoma, well created is Haoma, rightly created, properly created, healing, well formed, well working, victorious, freshly green, with pliant shoots. As is (best) for him who drinks it, so also it is the best provision for the soul. O Green One, I call*

---

[91] Indian Mythology, Knappert, 1991:235.

down your intoxication, your strength, victory, health, healing furtherance increase power for the whole body, ecstasy of all kinds... This boon I ask of you, O invincible Haoma! The Paradise of the just, light, encompassing all happiness. This second boon I ask of you, O invincible Haoma! Long life for its vital force. Haoma bestows strength and powers on those who swiftly pour... Haoma gives to nobly born women kingly progeny and just descendants... Hail to you, Haoma! Through your own strength you rule at will! Hail to you! You hearken to many words, (if) truly spoken."[92]

The first portion of any animal sacrifice was offered to the god Haoma. The priest would in that manner be caring for the animal's soul. Haoma as the god of health and strength and provider of rich harvests appeared to the prophet during the Haoma ceremony. Thus to the Zoroastrians Haoma will be present at every offering made by the faithful. At the end of the world Haoma will make all men immortal.

The classical Greek equivalent of the Norse Mani, god of the moon, is Artemis, goddess of the moon, also known as Cynthia, Pythia, and Phoebe. To the Romans the she was known as Diana. Artemis was the twin sister of Apollo the sun god, as the Norse sun goddess Sol was the sister to the moon god Mani.

Artemis was also the goddess of the hunt and childbirth. She was the goddess of virginity and was chaste. When Christianity subsumed the earlier pagan faiths the celibate Artemis became the Virgin Mary. As moon goddess she was associated with the night and the underworld controlled by Hades. She was depicted wearing a long robe reaching the floor with a veil. She had a crescent, representing her function as moon goddess on her head.

Ben Jonson, (1572-1637 CE) the English dramatist and poet gives a wonderful description in verse of this nocturnal moon goddess:

"Queen and huntress, chaste and fair,
Now the Sun is laid to sleep;

---

[92] Textual Sources for the Study of Zoroastrianism, Boyce (trans), 1984:55

Seated in thy silver chair,
State in wonted manner keep:
Hesperus entreats thy light,
Goddess excellently bright.

Earth, let not thy envious shade
Dare itself to interpose:
Cynthia's shining orb was made
Heaven to clear, when day did close;
Bless us then with wished sight,
Goddess excellently bright.

Lay thy bow of pearl apart,
And thy crystal-shining quiver;
Give unto the flying hart
Space to breathe, how short so ever:
Thou that mak'st a day of night,
Goddess excellently bright."[93]

As the classical Greeks had two sun gods, Apollo and Helios, so they also had two moon goddesses, Artemis and Selene. Selene was the daughter of the Titan, Hyperion and the sister of Helios. To the Romans she was the moon goddess Luna and her own temple on the Aventine Hill in Rome.

Interestingly Selene was depicted riding in a chariot driven by two horses. The Norse moon god, Mani also drives a chariot through the night sky.

There is a lovely story concerning Selene. She fell in love with Endymion, the king of Elis and bore him fifty daughters. Evidently when Endymion was sleeping he was seen by the moon goddess who then fell in love with him. She kissed him while he slept. This had a big effect on Endymion. Every night he was visited by the goddess. They fell in love. Zeus gave the love struck young man a choice, death or eternal sleep, Endymion chose eternal sleep so he could be with his beloved one, the goddess Selene.

This story became part of the folklore of Elis, a region in southern Greece in the north-west area of Peloponnese. The

---

[93] Every Man Out of His Humour, Cynthia's Revels and The Poetaster: The Works of Ben Jonson Part 2, Jonson & Gifford, 2004:361.

people became famous for their skills in horse breeding. In Ellis instead of saying that it was getting late, people would use the phrase: *"Selene loves and watches Endymion."* Similarly, instead of saying that the sun is setting and the moon is rising, the phrase: *"Selene embraces Endymion,"* would be used. Again, to say that there was night, the phrase would be: *"Selene kisses Endymion into sleep."*

In *Sexual Life in Ancient Greece*, by Hans Licht there is a fascinating ancient Greek charm which evokes the goddess Selene, which is taken from the *Greek Magical Papyri* (PGM IV.2441-2621):

> *"(Laudatory.) "Preparation of the smoke sacrifice that conjures up the moon-goddess. It brings hither without resistance and on the same day the soul (of the one to be charmed); it drives (the enemy) to the sick bed and surely kills; it sends blissful dreams and has shown itself effective in most enchantments. Pancrates the priest of Heliopolis, brought this offering before the emperor Hadrian and therewith proved to him the power of his divine magic; the spell followed in an hour, sickness in two, death in six hours, while he saw clearly and announced the enchantment that lay upon everything around him. Astounded at the prophet's art, he ordered a double honorarium to be given to him."*[94]

A shrewmouse is killed in spring-water, and two moon-headed beetles in running water. These are pounded in a pestle and mortar with a number of other ingredients to produce the offering. The other ingredients are a crawfish, fat from a speckled virgin goat, dung from a dog-headed ape, two ibis eggs two drachmae of Italic Alpine herb and two drachmae of incense and an onion without any sucker. The mixture is stored in a lead receptacle.

> *"When you want to use it, take some and go up to the loft with a coal-pan, and when the moon rises, offer the mixture with the following prayer, and Selene will immediately appear.*
>
> *(Prayer) "Let the gloomy veil of the clouds disperse above me and let the goddess Actiophis rise above me and listen to my holy prayer, for I have to disclose the insult of the shameful and impious N.N. (here the*

---

[94] Sexual Life in Ancient Greece, Licht, 2001:334.

enchanter inserts the name of the girl concerned). She has betrayed the holy mysteries to men. N.N. has also said: 'I saw the great goddess leave the vault of heaven and roam over the earth with naked feet, a sword in her hand, and silent.' N.N. also said : 'I saw how she drank blood.' N.N. said that; I did not. Actiophis Ereschigal Nebutosualethi Phophorbasa Tragiammon (magic names of the goddess, influenced by Oriental magic)! Betake thyself to N.N., deprive her of sleep. Throw the firebrand into her soul, and punish her with the unrest of madness, pursue her and bring her from every place and every house to me![95]

The offering is made with loud cries, and the spell caster then goes downstairs backwards and opens the door to let the soul of the person called escape from the wrathful goddess.

If now you wish to make anyone ill, use the same prayer and add: 'Make N.N., the daughter of N.N., sick.' If she is to die, then say: 'Take the breath, mistress from the nose of N.N.' If you wish to send a dream pray thus: 'Come to her in the form of the goddess, whom N.N. serves.' If you yourself desire a dream, then say: 'Come to me mistress, and give me during sleep advice on such and such a thing,' and she will come to you and tell you all without deception. But do not employ the charm too rashly, but only when you have a serious reason for it."[96]

That is an interesting and complicated rite for evoking the goddess and performing a magical ceremony. The ingredients alone, would take a lot of collecting. It explains how complex these rituals were, they were not to be taken lightly. But it also shows the power and respect in which the moon goddess Selene was held.

---

[95] Sexual Life in Ancient Greece, Licht, 2001:334.
[96] Sexual Life in Ancient Greece, Licht, 2001:335.

TUESDAY

Tuesday is the third day of the week. It was known to the Romans as *Dies Martis*, after Mars the god of war. Mars as a Greek and Roman god of war was often associated with the Norse god Tyr. To the Germanic nations it was *'Dingstag'*, or Court day. Many popular tribunals were held on that day. The Anglo-Saxons called it *Tiues-daeg* after Tiu, or Tyr, the Germanic and Norse god of war and the sky. Interestingly as it was originally a day for hearing legal complaints, Tyr has been considered a god of justice.

The *Edda* sings the praises of Tyr:

> *"There is a god called Tyr. He is the boldest and most courageous, and has the power over victory in battle; it is good for brave men to invoke him. It is a proverbial saying that he who surpasses others and does not waver is 'Tyr-valiant'. He is also so well informed that a very knowledgeable man is said to be 'Tyr-wise'."*[97]

Praise indeed, he was obviously held in very high esteem. Tyr was one of the twelve principle deities of Asgard. He was also known as Tiwaz, meaning *'god'*, Dyeus, Tiw, Tig or Teiwa. The parentage of this god is confused but he was thought to have been the son of the goddess Frigg, and the god Odin; though in some myths he is said to be the son of the giant Hymir.

Tyr appears to be equated with the Saxon god Saxnot (or Saxneat). Saxnot is mentioned as being one of the deities to be renounced along with the better known Woden and Thunor at Christian baptisms. This seems to be one of the many ancient gods who have now disappeared from memory. As Saxneat he was the founder of the Saxon royal dynasty in Essex. So at one time he must have been an important god. The name derives from *'sahsginot'* meaning companion of the sword. Sax itself means *'a sword'*. Saxnot is thought to be a local form of Tyr. Many gods in those days were known in

---

[97] The Prose Edda of Snorri Sturluson, Young, 1964:53.

different areas by different names. Each tribe might have a different name for the same god. Many of the deities equated with Tyr are associated with swords.

Another of these local divinities associated with Tyr was Cheru, the chief divinity of the tribe of the Cheruski. Here he was a god of the sun, with his shining sword blade an emblem of the sun's rays.

There is a wonderful story attached to Cheru's sword. This was a magical weapon, which had been made by dwarves. Whoever wielded it in battle would not lose. It was kept in a sacred temple, positioned so that it reflected the first beams of the sun in the morning. But this holy sword disappeared. The prophetess of the temple said that whoever wielded this sword would conquer the world but come to his death by it.

Vitellius, a Roman prefect, was given this sword and told that it would bring him glory and he would become an emperor. Duly Vitellius was elected Emperor of Rome. However Vitellius did not look after the magical sword. A German soldier took, it replacing it with his own rusty blade. Vitellius went to Rome to be proclaimed Emperor. There he got a shock; the Eastern Roman Legions had named Vespasian emperor. Vitellius searched in vain for his sword to save him. But it was too late. He was seized by the population and dragged to the bottom of the Capitoline Hill. Here the German soldier cut off Vitellius head with the sacred sword. The prophecy was fulfilled.

The soldier buried the magical sword in the earth. He guarded it while he lived. But he would never reveal its resting place only saying that it would be found by the man destined to conquer the world. Here it lay. The years passed.

Attila, called the *'Scourge of God'*, and the leader of a ferocious band of warriors called the Huns was passing along a river. He met a peasant who was examining the foot of a cow, wounded by something sharp hidden in the grass. When Attila investigated he found a buried sword. This he declared was Cheru's sword, brandishing it over his head; he would now conquer the world. Battle after battle was won by Attila. He settled in Hungary, tired from constant fighting. He took as a wife the beautiful Burgundian princess Ildico. But he had murdered the princess's father, and she wanted revenge. Attila got drunk on his wedding night, and Ildico, seizing her chance, took the sword and killed him in his own bed. The prophecy was fulfilled once more.

The mystical sword once again disappeared. The last time it was used was by the Duke of Alva, the general of Charles V, who won the victory of Muhlberg in 1547 CE. The Franks went on to win many battles.

But by now the sword had lost its pagan connotations. The old gods were renounced. The sword was now dedicated to the Archangel St. Michael. And this is how it is known today. So yet another bit of pagan mythology was Christianised to fit the new religious beliefs.

Ziu, Zio Ziumen or Ziu-Wari were the names of another Germanic local god equated with Tiwaz or Tyr. This was from the Swabian or Suabian tribe. They called their capital Ziusburg, this is modern Augsburg in the Baltic area of Germany. Again there is this connection with the sword as this god had the emblem of this weapon. There were special sword dances held in his honour. The dancers would stand in two long lines crossing their swords with the point upright. Now the dancers would jump over the swords. It must have been a very spectacular dance. The Suabians had another sword dance that they performed. Here they joined their sword points closely together in the shape of a rose or wheel. Now the chief of the tribe would stand on this platform of shining steel blades and be carried aloft on it through the camp in triumph. That must have been an impressive sight. To the Suabians the sword was so sacred that oaths were sworn on it.

Tyr was worshipped between 500 BCE, if not even earlier through to 1100 CE. Rather bloody sacrifices were offered to Tyr by the Franks and other northern nations. The Germanic Hermundurii tribe offered human sacrifices to Tyr. The priests called Godi, offered human sacrifices to Tyr on alters. Here prisoners of war were spread eagled. That is to say they cut on either side of the backbone, and their ribs were turned inside out. The internal organs then torn out of the body. It was considered honourable to endure this without making a sound. That is bravery. These sacrifices were made on dolmens throughout Northern Europe.

Figure 16 - Tyr

Runic symbols of Tyr have been found on spears as a talismanic protection, Tyr being the god of bravery. Tyr was also patron god of the sword and runes were carved on every blade. Here is the description of these protection runes from the *Lay of Sigdrifa*:

"*Sig-runes thou must know,*
If victory thou wilt have,
And on thy sword's hilt rist them;
Some on the chapes,
Some on the guard,
And twice name the name of Tyr."[98]

The gods to the Germanic and Northern people were not always whole. Tyr had only one hand, in fact he was known as *'hinn eindendi ass'*, the one-handed god. This could be symbolic of the fact that he would only give victory to one side in a battle. Another theory is that as Tyr's symbol is a sword, and a sword only has but one blade.

But according to Norse myth there was a reason why he was so deformed. One of the god Loki's children was a demonic wolf, Fenrir. The gods brought this wolf home. A ferocious beast, only Tyr was brave enough to feed it. The wolf grew fast into a large monster. The gods were scared for it was said that this beast would one day cause them harm. So they chained the wolf, but with every strong and powerful iron chain placed over it, the animal just shook himself free. They tried two chains, Laeding and Droma, each stronger than the last. But neither were tough enough. The gods got worried, this was not working. There are a couple of proverbs common in the North that are used: *'to get loose out of Laeding,'* and *'to dash out of Droma'*. Both of these are figurative expression used whenever great difficulties have to be surmounted.

So the gods asked the dwarves for help. The dwarves made a slender ribbon. This was a magical ribbon called Gleipnir. The wolf turned its nose up at being incarcerated by such a feeble ribbon. He said:
"This ribbon looks to me as if I could gain no renown from breaking it - it is so slight a cord; but if it has been

---

98 The Norsemen (Myths and Legends), Guerber, 1994:86.

*made by guile and cunning, slender thought it looks, it
is not going to come on my legs."*[99]

So the wolf refused. The gods now replied:

*"and if you don't succeed in snapping this cord you
need not be afraid of the gods; we will set you free
again." The wolf replied:*

*"If you bind me so that I can't get free, then you will
sneak away so that it will be a long time before I get
any help from you, I don't want to have that ribbon put
on me. But rather than be accused of cowardice by
you, let one of you place his hand in my mouth as a
pledge that this is done in good faith."*[100]

None of the gods were willing to put this to the test.
Except that is the brave Tyr. Tyr boldly placed his right hand
in the mouth of the massive wolf. The wolf now struggled
hard to free himself from the bounds of the magical ribbon.
But, unlike the iron chains, it would not shatter. The harder
the wolf tried to get free the more the massive jaws closed
round Tyr's hand. Poor Tyr lost his hand. That was the price
for enclosing the wolf. A truly courageous god Tyr had acted
on his principles. However Tyr still continued to fight. He
wielded his shield on his maimed right arm, and used his
sword in his left hand, where it proved to be lethal to
adversaries.

There are parallels between the one handed Tyr and
Nuada of the Silver Hand in Irish Celtic mythology. Nuada
was also known as Nudd of the Silver Hand in the Welsh
Celtic tradition. Nuada was Nuada Argetlamh, leader of the
gods. Like Tyr he had a sword from which none could
escape. He was the first ruler of the magical Tuatha De
Danann, the people of the goddess Dana. They were gods of
light and righteousness and fought their ancient enemies the
Firbolgs, the gods of darkness. Nuada led the Tuatha De
Danann while the Firbolgs were led by their king, mac Erc.
The two opposing sides met at the Plain of Moytura, the
Plain of the Towers. This became known as the first battle of
Magh Tuireadh. The fighting was bitter, but the Danann won
and mac Erc was slain. But the price was high, Nuada lost

---

[99] The Prose Edda of Snorri Sturluson, Young, 1964:58.

his hand. It was replaced by a silver one made by the Celtic god of medicine, Dian Cecht. After the battle the Firbolgs were allotted the province of Connacht, while the rest of Ireland was given to the Danann. Even as late as the seventeenth century many of the people of Connacht traced their ancestry to the Firbolgs.

Tyr himself is an ancient god of the sky. The name can be equated with the Latin *deus*, Old Irish *dia*, Sanskrit *Deva* and the Old Norse plural *tivar*. Now these are all forms of saying god. Tyr is said to have derived from an older god *Tiwaz*. It is clear that Tyr was an ancient and prominent god, having a high position in the Norse hierarchy, although like many other ancient deities his name and importance has been lost in the mists of time. In fact the theory is that once he was the All-father before being ousted by Odin.

---

[100] Ibid, 1964:58.

WEDNESDAY

Wednesday is the fourth day of the week. The Romans called it *Dies Mercurii*, Mercury's Day. In France this day is called Mercredi after Mercury. Mercury was mainly a god of trade and commerce and thieves, as well as a messenger of the gods to the Romans. That throws light on what the Romans thought of merchants, perhaps they were not very honest in their dealings. Mercury had other functions. He was also known as Psychopompus, meaning leader of souls, in which role he led the souls of the dead to Hades, the Roman underworld. It was in this last function that he corresponded to the Saxon god Woden. Woden also led souls. After battle he would take them to Valhalla, the Norse Underworld. The day became Wodnes-deag, or Woden's Day becoming Wednesday. Woden is perhaps better known as his Norse equivalent Odin. This is interesting as Odin is usually thought to be the head of the gods. If it had been during this period in history he would have been given the fifth day of the week which was the Roman god Jove's day, their own king of the gods. There does appear to be controversy to which god actually was the main Norse deity.

Kemble's *Solomon and Saturn* offers another explanation for the linking of Woden to Mercury:

> *"Once there lived a man who was Mercury called;*
> *he was vastly deceitful and cunning in his deeds,*
> *he loved well to steal and all lying tricks;*
> *the heathens had made him the highest of their gods,*
> *and at the cross-roads they offered him booty*
> *and to the high hills brought him victims to slay.*
> *This god was the most honoured among all the heathen;*
> *his name when translated to Danish is Odin."*[101]

Here Mercury's role as god of liars and thieves is expressed. There is a story in Greek mythology that relates

---

[101] The Lost Gods of England, Branston, 1993:96.

how Mercury stole cattle from Apollo. Mercury was dragged off to Olympus by the angry Apollo and there was found guilty of his crime. He was ordered to replace the oxen he had taken. To replace the two that he had eaten Mercury gave Apollo a lyre. But after that Mercury was god of liars and thieves and vagabonds. Perhaps these qualities were admired by the Norse who were a warlike and pillaging people and they associated them with Odin.

To Snorri Odin was an important god. He was called the All-father and father of the gods. He was also known as Valfather meaning *'father of the slain'* as all those who fall in battle were regarded as his sons. These fallen soldiers were sent to Valhalla and Vingolf where they were called the Einherjar, meaning *'belonging to an army'* or *'the Champions'*. These would fight again at the end of the world at Ragnarok.

Odin had many names which Snorri quotes. Here I will reproduce them together with their meaning, where given. I have also added some of the meanings of the names from *The Dictionary of Norse Myth and Legend*, by Andy Orchard:

Hangagud	*God of the hanged*
Haptagud	*God of the gods*
Farmagud	*God of cargoes*
Grim	*Masked One*
Gangleri	*Wanderer*
Herjan	*Raider*
Hjalmberi	*Helmeted One*
Thekk	*Pleasant One*
Thridi	*Third*
Thud	*Thin One*
Ud	*Lover? Beloved? Striver?*
Helblindi	*One who blinds with death*
Har	*High One*
Svipall	*Changeable One*
Sanngetall	*One who guesses right*
Herteit	*Glad of war*
Hnikar	*(Spear) thruster*
Bileyg	*One whose eye deceives him; One-eyed*
Baleyg	*Flame eyed One*
Bolverk	*Worker of Evil*
Fjolnir	*Much-wise? Concealer?*
Grimnir	*Masked One*
Glapsvid	*Seducer*

Fjolsvid	*Very wise One*
Sidhott	*Deep hooded One*
Sidskegg	*Long bearded One*
Sigfod	*Father of battle*
Hnikud	*(Spear) thruster*
Allfod	*All father*
Atrid	*Attacking Rider*
Farmatyr	*Cargo god*
Oski	*Fulfiller of desire*
Omi	*Boomer*
Jafnhar	*Just as high*
Biflindi	*Blind*
Gondlir	*Wand-wielder*
Harbard	*Grey bearded One*
Svdur	*Calmer? Spear-god?*
Svidir	*Calmer? Spear-god?*
Jark	*Gelding*
Kjalar	*Nourisher*
Vidur	*Killer?*
Ygg	*Terrible One*
Thund	*Rumbler*
Vak	*Alert One*
Vafud	*Dangler*
Hroptatyr	*Lord of Gods? Tumult-god?*
Gaut	*One from Gotland, Gaut, Goth*
Veratyr	*God of men*

That is an awful lot of names. But generally Odin was known as the All-father. Here is Snorri's description of the great god:

> *"He lives for ever and ever, and rules over the whole of his kingdom and governs all things great and small...He created heaven and earth and the sky and all that in them is...His greatest achievement, however, is the making of man and giving him a soul which will live and never die, although his body may decay to dust or burn to ashes. All righteous men shall live and be with him where it is called Gimle (Lee of fire) or Vingolf (Friendly floor) but wicked men will go to Hel and thence to Niflhel (Abode of darkness) that is down in the ninth world."*[102]

---

[102] The Prose Edda of Snorri Sturluson, Young, 1964:31.

This sounds a very Christian description of the Norse heathen god, with its echoes of immortality. A lot of ancient myth was later Christianised as the older religions lost their supremacy over the people.

Odin is generally depicted a being a tall vigorous and muscular man aged about fifty. He had dark curly hair or sometimes a bald head with a long grey beard. He was dressed in grey and blue, symbolic of the sky and clouds. Odin generally wore a grey tunic with a blue hood and mantle, the latter being flecked with grey. His head gear varied. When he visited battle fields on earth or seated upon his mighty throne he wore a gold helmet with an eagle on it. An ornate helmet was found as part of the Sutton Hoo ship burial. But sometimes he visited the world of man incognito, then he would wear a simple broad brimmed hat which concealed the fact that he had only one eye.

Odin had three wives. The first was called Jord, an earth goddess. Jord was the daughter of night or according to another myth, the giantess Fiorgyn. It was from the union of these two that there was the god Thor, the god of thunder, and from whom Thursday was named. Odin's second and principle wife was Frigg, the Queen of the gods. Odin and Frigg produced Baldur, the god of spring, Hermod, messenger of the gods, and Tyr, the god of war and from whom Tuesday got its name. His third wife was Rind. Rind was the goddess of the harsh and frozen cold soil. She gave birth to Vali who was bold in battle and a very good shot.

Odin was involved with other women. There was Saga, the goddess of history. It is from her that we have the verb 'to say'. Odin would visit her every day for a drink in her crystal hall, Sokkvabekk. Then there was the giantess Grid. From her there was the god Vidor one of the few survivors of Ragnarok, the end of the world. There was the giantess Gunnlod. She was seduced by Odin who wanted the mead of poetry. Together they conceived Bragi, the god of music poetry and eloquence.

Odin had a magical throne called Hlidskjalf, from here he could see the whole world. Turnville-Petre gives an interesting interpretation of the name. *Hlid* means 'an opening or gap'. The second part of the name *skjalf* means 'a steep slope' or 'a cutting off of a high plateau'. In Old English this last part of Hlidskjalf, corresponds to *scelf* or *scylf*, meaning crag or rock. He says that perhaps the meaning of this special seat in which Odin sat was *'the hill, rock with an opening in it'*. In other words, Odin was looking through an opening between his world and the world of men.

He has two ravens which sit on his shoulder. They are called Hugin, meaning *'Thought'* and Munin, meaning *'Memory'*. These birds played an important role for Odin. Every morning the ravens would be sent out and return later at dinner. They would fly all round the world and report back to Odin everything they had seen. So Odin was well informed. Here is the description from Snorri's *Edda*:

> *"Over the world*
> *every day*
> *fly Hugin and Munin;*
> *I fear that Hugin*
> *will not come back,*
> *though I'm more concerned about Munin."*[103]

Ravens were associated with Odin and he was known as god of ravens. Some of Odin's many names concur with this, he was called Hrafnass, *'raven-god'*; Hrafnfreistudr, *'raven-tempter'*; and Hrafnblots godi, *'the priest of the raven-sacrifice'*.

The raven itself is linked with death. They prey on bodies on the battlefield. Odin himself is linked with battles and warfare. There is vivid imagery here of ravens feeding off the corpses of dead warriors.   Odin was god of war and death. The raven became known as a predictor of victor as the birds would amass waiting for a feast of bodies slain by the victor. From this it was but a small step for the raven to be seen as a lucky bird that would assure victory. That is why ravens appear on so many battle standards.

Odin is also associated with the wolf. He had two wolves called Geri, meaning *'Greedy'* and Freki, meaning *'Gluttonous'*. These animals he fed with raw meat from his own table as Odin himself did not eat food and lived on wine. This is described by Snorri:

---

[103] The Prose Edda of Snorri Sturluson, Young, 1964:64.

Figure 17 - Hugin and Munin

"Battle-wont and famous,
Odin war-glorious,
sates Geri and Freki;
the Father-of-armies
himself lives always
only on wine."[104]

Wolves like ravens are associated with death. Both animals haunt battlefields feeding off the dead. Sometimes the wolf is called *'Odin's dog'*, or *'Vidris grey'*. In many ancient cultures wolves and hounds are interchangeable, both symbolic of the war and death.

Another animal Odin was linked with was the horse. He had a magical grey steed called Sleipnir with eight legs. The parentage of this mystical horse is strange. It came from a stallion called Svadilfari and the god Loki. Evidently Loki being a shape-changer had taken the form of a mare and after making love to the stallion had bore this remarkable beast. Sleipnir could gallop very fast over all the Norse nine worlds. Odin's horse could travel through the air and over the sea. Snorri says that: *"among gods and men that horse is the best"*. Praise indeed.

Horses are symbolic of fertility. Fertility with its themes of birth and rebirth is often linked with death. Odin appears to have a lot of imagery associated with death. This death theme is repeated in Norse verse. In the saga *Ynglinga Tal*, the gallows are described as the *"high-chested rope Sleipnir"*,[105] *habrjostr horva Sleipnir*, in the native tongue. Here again are more portrayals of death, Odin and the horse. This is confirmed in archaeological finds. Hundreds of horses have been found buried in graves throughout Scandinavia. In one grave alone, that of the Oseberg, sixteen horses were exhumed.

The horse appears to have many connections with death. In Scottish folklore the Kelpie was a water horse who would lure unsuspecting folk on to its back and then gallop into water and their rider would be drowned. In classical mythology Diomedes, king of the Bistones of Thrace fed his

---

[104] Ibid, 1964:63
[105] Myth and Religion of the North, Turnville-Petre, 1975:56.

horses on passing strangers. Diomedes though was killed by Hercules, who in turn fed his body to the hungry horses.

The bible continues this theme of horse and death. In *Revelations 6:8* there is *"I looked and behold a pale horse: and his name that sat on him was death, and Hell followed with him."*

Many folklore stories relate to the horse or someone riding a horse being a premonition of death.

Odin had a magical spear called Gungnir. This remarkable spear once thrown always reached its aim. One of the many names of Odin was *'Lord of the Spear'*. It was forged by the dwarves and was so sacred that if an oath had been sworn on its point it could not be broken. Gungnir was a symbol of Odin's power.

Odin also had a magical gold arm ring called Draupnir. This was forged by the dwarves Brokk and Sindri. Every ninth night this ring would spawn another eight rings each as heavy as the first. Rings are an ancient fertility symbol, they are circular and as such symbolise eternal life, birth, death and rebirth. This is emphasised in the fact that from Draupnir emerges new rings, identical to the original.

Odin was the god of wind. As such the one eyed god was often pictured flying through the air on his magical steed the eight legged Sleipnir. Thus there is an old Northern riddle:

> *"Who are the two who ride to the Thing?*
> *Three eyes have they together, ten feet, and one tail:*
> *and thus they travel through the lands."*[106]

Odin was associated with death and was leader of disembodied spirits. What with this and his link with the wind, it was a terrifying combination. He was thought to pick up dead spirits, mount them on horses and fly with them through the air accompanied by baying hounds. On a dark, windy, stormy night the roaring wind was thought to represent Odin and ghost hunters. This was known as the Wild Hunt and Odin was the Wild Huntsman. It was bad luck to see the hunt, for it meant that you would be carried to a distant land. To see the Huntsman himself was certain death.

---

[106] The Norsemen (Myths and Legends), Guerber, 1994:25.

There is a description of the Wild Hunt in the Laud version of the *Anglo-Saxon Chronicle* for 1127 CE:

> *"Let no one be surprised at the truth of what we are about to relate, for it was general knowledge throughout the whole country that immediately after his arrival - it was the Sunday (6th February) when they sing Exurge Quare o(bdormis), D(omine) - many men both saw and heard a great number of huntsmen hunting. The huntsmen were black huge, and hideous, and rode on black horses and on black he-goats, and their hounds were jet black, with eyes like saucers, and horrible. This was seen in the very deer park of the town of Peterborough, and in all the woods that stretch from that same town to Stamford, and in the night the monks heard them sounding and winding their horns. Reliable witnesses who kept watch in the night declared that there might well have been as many as twenty or thirty of them winding their horns as near as they could tell. This was seen and heard from the time of his arrival all through Lent and right up to Easter. Such was his entrance: of his exit we cannot yet say. Let it be as God ordains!"*[107]

Myths abound about the Wild Hunt. If you joined the hunt in mockery, you would be hoisted up and whirled away with the rest of the lost souls. If you joined the hunt in seriousness, you would be rewarded by a horse's leg hurled from the sky. In the morning this leg would metamorphose into a lump of gold.

A small black dog was sometimes left by the hunt as it swept through the sky. The poor animal would cower and whimper. The dog was kept and fed for a year unless exorcised. It would be exorcised by an old recipe. Beer would be brewed in egg shells and the animal fed the resulting liquid. This had the strange effect of making the dog fly with his tail between his legs. Evidently it looked an odd sight.

This connection between the hunt and dogs continued in the tradition of Gabriel's hound. Or Gabble Ratchet or Wild Geese. Here it was said that the sound of a flock of geese was similar to that of a pack of hounds in full flight. The myth was now Christianised that the tormented souls flying

---

[107] The Anglo-Saxon Chronicle, Garmonsway (trans), 1975:258.

through the night were the souls of unbaptised children roaming through the air, doomed to stay there until the Day of Judgement. Anyone hearing the sound of these eerie hounds would be either condemned to die or there would be a death of someone close to them.

There is a similar tradition in Dartmoor. The Wish Hounds or Yell Hounds would terrorise the area on moonless nights. They would be led by the Midnight Hunter of the Moor, who rode a huge horse that breathes fire and flame. These hounds, sometimes said to be headless, roam above an ancient track called the Abbot's Way. Again there is the saying that to hear the animals means certain death.

Different versions of this tale abounded. Sometimes imaginary animals such as boars or wild horses flew through the air. Sometimes there were white breasted maidens or wood nymphs. These nymphs were called Moss Maidens. They symbolised the autumn leaves discarded from the trees and blown by the winds.

Through the years the leader of the hunt changed too. Now it was no longer Odin who terrorised the neighbourhood. It was Charlemagne, Frederick Barbarossa, Herold, Cain or even King Arthur.

The hunt was usually heard during the period between Christmas and Twelfth Night and it became customary to leave out the last sheaf or measure of grain in the fields to feed Odin's hungry horse.

Different versions of this theme of the Wild Hunt are common in Europe. Even as late as the eve of the French Revolution, the shout of the hunt was heard in the sky.

There is a strange story of Odin choosing to hang for nine days and nights from the sacred ash tree Yggdrasil. He pieced himself with a spear and cried out with pain. This is interesting as Odin is the god of the dead and of the hanged. In fact he is called the 'lord of the gallows', and 'god of the hanged'. He died as a sacrifice to himself.

Here is the ancient Norse description of Odin's penance on Yggdrasil related in Branston's *Gods of the North*:

> "I'm aware that I hung
> on a windy tree, swung there nights all of nine:
> gashed with a blade
> bloodied for Odin, myself an offering to myself
> knotted to that tree

no man knows whither the root of it runs.

None gave me bread,
none gave me drink, down to the depths I peered
to snatch up runes
with a roaring screech and fall in a dizzied faint!

Wellbeing I won
and wisdom too, I grew and joyed in my growth;
from a word to a word
I was led to a word from a deed to another deed."[108]

There are parallel here between Odin and Christ. Both die voluntary, both are pierced with a spear, both die hanging Christ from a cross, Odin from a holy tree, neither the cross nor the tree had roots, and both cry out before dying. The similarities are striking.

While hanging on Yggdrasil Odin learned the wisdom of the runes. There were eighteen of these runes and from them Odin learnt many things. He now had the knowledge to heal, blunt or break metal, to avert evil intentions, douse flames, calm stormy water, seduce, send witches into a spin and to speak to hanged men. Odin was now enlightened. He carved these runes on his spear Gungnir, and the teeth of his horse Sleipnir. Odin was now always associated with the hanged and the gallows.

There is an interesting story as to how Odin lost his eye. He visited Mimir's spring. This spring was under the root of the sacred tree Yggdrasil. All wisdom was stored in this hallowed spring. The owner Mimir, which means memory, himself was full of enlightenment from drinking water from this holy spring. Odin asks for a drink of this precious water. But this is not granted unless he gave a sacrifice. Odin was asked to donate one of his most precious possessions, his eye. This he gladly did as he wanted the secrets of the water.

Mimir took the eye and placed it in the liquid. The eye disappeared from sight. Here is Snorri's description:

"I know for certain Odin
where you concealed your eye,
in the famous

---

[108] Gods of the North, Branston, 1955:115.

Figure 18 - Odin's Sacrifice

spring of Mimir;
mead he drinks
every morning
from the pledge of the Father of the Slain.
Do you know any more or not?"[109]

Odin drank deeply the magical liquid. He now had
mystical wisdom he desired but he had lost an eye. The
theme of sacrifice is common in many ancient cultures, the
more the gain, the greater the sacrifice. Odin was now one
eyed which is considered symbolic of the sun.

Odin was now master of magic. He could practice *galdr*
magic and also the baser form called *seidr*. Now he could see
into the future, cause death misfortune and sickness and
cause men to go mad. Powerful magic indeed! Seidr was
normally only practised by the goddess, it was considered a
female art. For Odin to master it was strange because it was
held to be dishonourable for the male sex. Seidr was
accompanied by practices that were considered depraved
such as homosexuality, witchcraft and cowardice. These
things were not considered appropriate for men to do, they
were called *'ergi'*.

This is bizarre as Odin was a war god. He could blind,
deafen and strike terror into his enemies. He could blunt
their weapons so as they became as worthless as sticks.
Odin's own fighters were as savage as wolves and as strong
as bulls. He was a very strong warlike figure for the martial
Norse and Viking plunderers of the age.

There is also a tradition of Odin as a semi-historical
figure. This Odin was considered to be the leader of a tribe
from Asia Minor, known as the Aesir, who left their land after
being threatened by the Romans in 70 CE. Men, women,
young and old, took their valuables and migrated with him
to Europe. He conquered Russia, Germany, Denmark,
Norway, and Sweden, a truly massive empire. He left one of
his sons on each throne to defend the country. Vegdeg had
East Germany, Beldeg also known as Baldr had Westphalia,
and Sigi and his son Renir had France. Odin's son Skjold
governed Reidgotaland which became Jutland. The family
later became kings of Denmark. Another of Odin's sons and

---

[109] The Prose Edda of Snorri Sturluson, Young, 1964:43.

his son, Saeming ruled Norway. Yet another of Odin's sons called Yngvi ruled Sweden. Thus all the ruling families of Scandinavia trace their roots back to the god Odin.

The tracing of the royalty to Odin is echoed in England. The country was invaded by the Jutes, Angles and Saxons in the fifth century. These were known as the *'three tribes of Germany'* and were Germanic people who traced their descent back to Odin or his English equivalent Woden. This is confirmed in the Parker version of the *Anglo-Saxon Chronicle*:

> *"In the year of Christ's Nativity 494, Cerdic and Cynric his son landed at Cerdicesora with five ships. That Cerdic was the son of Elesa, the son of Esla, the son of Gewis, the son of Wig, the son of Freawine, the son of Frithugar, the son of Brand, the son of Baeldeag, the son of Woden."*[110]

The *Chronicle* then relates that six years after they landed they captured the kingdom of Wessex. Thus the kings of Wessex can date back to Woden.

Again this is echoed by the *Chronicle*. Hengest and Horsa who led the Anglo Saxon invasions of the country descended from Woden. Hengest and his brother Horsa, their names meaning *'gelding'* and *'horse'* respectively, seized Kent. Kent's kings claimed descent through Aesc or Oisc, Hengist's son and back from him to Woden.

In 626 CE the Parker version of the *Anglo-Saxon Chronicle* traces Penda, King of Mercia back to Woden:

> *"Penda was the son of Pybba, the son of Croda, the son of Cynewald, the son of Cnebba, the son of Icel, the son of Eomer, the son of Angeltheow, the son of Offa, the son of Wermund, the son of Wihtlaeg, the son of Woden."*[111]

It is from a different son of Woden, but the Mercians, like the kings of Wessex and Kent all traced their roots back to the All-father Odin.

---

[110] The Anglo-Saxon Chronicle, Garmonsway (trans), 1975:2.
[111] Ibid, 1975:24.

THURSDAY

Thursday is the fifth day of the week. To the Romans it was *Dies Jovis*, Jove's Day. This was changed to the Norse and Germanic god Thor, becoming Thor's day or Thursday. Jove is another name for Jupiter, the Roman sky god and god of the weather. As controller of the weather Jupiter sent lightning, thunder, and rain. Thor was also a god of weather. He was the Norse god of war and a sky god, and like Jupiter controlled storms and thunder. He was worshipped until 1100 CE or even later.

The similarities between Thor and Jove are echoed in the tenth century verse from Kemple's *Solomon and Saturn*:

> *"This Jove is most worshipped of all the gods,*
> *that the heathens had in their delusion;*
> *his name is Thor among some peoples;*
> *and the Danish nation love him best of all."*[112]

Thor is also known as Thunor or Donar. He was the son of Odin and Jord, sometimes known as Erda, the earth goddess. Thor is described by Snorri in the *Edda*:

> *"Thor, who is called Asa-Thor or Thor-the-charioteer, is the foremost of them (the gods). He is the strongest of all gods and men. He rules over that kingdom called Thrudvangar (Plains-of-power), and his hall is called Bilshirnir (strong); in that building are six hundred and forty floors - it is the largest house known to men."*[113]

Thor was tall and muscular. He had red hair and beard. When in a rage showers of sparks flew around. It was not good to anger him. He wore a broad brimmed hat, and because of this in Sweden storm clouds are known as Thor's hat. Here is a wonderful description of the great god himself from the *Valhalla*:

> *"First, Thor with the bent brow,*
> *In the red beard muttering low,*

---

[112] The Lost Gods of England, Branston, 1993:112.
[113] The Prose Edda of Snorri Sturluson, Young, 1964:50.

Darting fierce lightnings from eyeballs that glow,
Comes, while each chariot wheel
Echoes in thunder peal,
as his dread hammer shock
Makes Earth and Heaven rock,
Clouds rifting above, while Earth quakes below."[114]

Interestingly the Hindus also have a god equated with Jupiter, this is Brihaspati sometimes called Brhaspati, the Lord of Prayer. He drives a chariot drawn by eight horses. Like Thor's double headed axe of hammer the magical Mjollnir, Brihaspati is associated with a golden axe. Thor was a god of light and fire, similarly Brihaspati as the planet Jupiter was called the *'gold-coloured one'* or the *'shining one'*. Again like Thor this Hindu deity rules Thursday.

Thor must have been an impressive sight to behold, very awe inspiring. He also had a crown. On each point of this crown was a glittering star or burning flame. Fire was the element symbolic to Thor. His head was therefore surrounded by a halo of fire or light. This is interesting because Christ and his disciples are always shown with a halo of light around their head.

Thor's chariot was noisy and the rumble and roar of the thunder was said to be the roll of his chariot. In Southern Germany this tumultuous chariot was said to be furnished with copper kettles. These kettles rattled and clattered. This earned Thor the nickname the kettle vendor.

Thor's special chariot was pulled by two goats. These were called *Tooth-gnasher* and *Gap tooth*. From the teeth and hoofs of these two animals there were constant bright glowing sparks. One of the stories about Thor concerns these goats. He was travelling in his chariot with Loki, when they came across a poor peasant's hut. They decided to stop and have something to eat. But the peasant farmer, his wife and two children Thialfi and Roskva were impoverished and the family were hungry. However they saw that they had two very eminent visitors and they offered the gods full hospitality. The family had no food for themselves never mind their guests, but they offered them everything that they had. The gods were welcome to dine on potage and

---

[114] The Norsemen (Myths and Legends), Guerber, 1994:56.

vegetables. The household could not even offer them a chicken for there was no meat to be had.

Thor took pity on the poor farming family. He killed his two goats to provide dinner for all. But there was a proviso, which was that all the goats' bones should be thrown unbroken, onto the goatskins on the floor. But the son Thialfi, was too hungry, and he gnawed a thigh bone. Eagerly devouring the rich marrow he threw the discarded bone with the others hoping that the god would not notice.

In the morning the gods were ready to depart. Thor waved his magic hammer over the goat skin and bones. The goats were resurrected and given new life. They were now full of life and bleating. But something was wrong. One of them was lame. Thor was livid with rage. His temper was intense. His command had been disregarded. The family quaked in fear; they thought that they would be killed. You do not anger the gods. Thialfi admitted what he had done. The farmer, distraught, offered Thor everything he owned just to save their lives. Thor relented, but he took the farmers children, both his son Thialfi and his daughter Roskva to serve him forever.

Goats were often used in various ancient mythologies. To the ancient Greeks the she goat symbolised lightning which of course is associated with Thor, god of weather. There is also the story of the Greek goat, Amalthea. Zeus, the king of gods, broke one its horns. This horn became the cornucopia, the horn of plenty, the horn of Amalthea. This magical horn gave its owner whatever it desired. The goat was then set in sky as a constellation.

Goats were also associated with plenty and sacred to Faunus, Greek god of agriculture, and Dionysus, the Greek god of wine and fertility. Dionysus was sometimes known as 'kid' and at Athens and Hermion he was worshipped as 'the one of the Black Goatskin'. In fact according to legend Dionysus was turned into a goat by Zeus. Allied to these gods were the mythical beings the Greek Satyrs, and the Roman Fauns, Pans, and Sylvans. These strange creatures had human torsos, arms, and heads, but the lower part of their bodies were like goats. They also had short goat like horns on their heads. These odd animals were very lecherous and fond of their wine. They were highly sexual, again symbolic of plenty.

There is a Hindu prescription for an aphrodisiac concerning the goat. A liquid is prepared by boiling milk and sugar with the testicle of a goat or ram.

There are many strange legends concerning goats. It was said that they breathed through their horns. Pliny said that they were continually feverish. Goat's blood was said to be able to temper steel. The blood was supposed to have miraculous properties. In Southern India, the Kuruvikkarans, a class of bird catchers and beggars, believe that the wisdom of the goddess Kali is evoked by a priest after he drinks the blood from the throat of a freshly cut goat. Here is Pliny the Elder in his book *Natural History*, on the special properties of goats:

> "*Drusus, while tribune of the people, is reported to have drunk goat's blood because he wished, by his paleness, to accuse his enemy Quintus Caepio of having poisoned him and so to arouse hatred against him. So great is the power of he-goat's blood that its use in tempering gives a finer edge than any other method, and a rough surface is smoothed more thoroughly by it than by a file.*"[115]

Goats were also thought to act as guardians of a village. They absorbed disease and evil influences. The goat also acted as a lightning conductor deflecting bad luck. Its efficiency was said to have been gauged by the length of its beard and the rankness of its smell. Evidently a strong smelling he-goat was an excellent protector. Every village had a he-goat as a guardian.

Thor had three great treasures. The first was a magical hammer called Mjollnir, meaning '*Crusher*'. It was specially made for him by the dwarf Sindri. This implement he would hurl at his enemies, the frost giants. The hammer once thrown always returned back into Thor's hand like a boomerang.

This mighty hammer was the emblem of the thunderbolts that Thor threw. The hammer is sometimes depicted as a double sided axe, also a fertility symbol. The

---

[115] Natural History, Pliny the Elder, 1991:257.

axe is sometimes associated with Thor. When Mjollnir was thrown there were often divine fire and rain to accompany the weapon. This hammer is considered a fertility symbol. It was used to hallow or bless a bride in one of the sagas by being placed on the knees of the newly married woman. This hallowing of marriage by the hammer of Thor continued until Christian times. Echoes of the custom were seen in couples eloping to be married under the anvil in Gretna Green.

In other sagas the religious significance of Thor's hammer is stressed. It blessed a new born child and hallowed the dead in yet another tale. The Mjollnir appears to symbolise not only violence but also fertility and rebirth.

This hammer was very sacred. The Norse often made the sign of the hammer, in the same way that Christians later made the sign of the cross. It was used as a sign to ward off evil spirits. In a similar ceremony to Christian baptism the sign of the hammer was made over new born babies who then had their heads wetted with water when they were given their name. A sacred hammer was used to drive boundary stakes to mark out territory. These stakes could not now be moved, for to do so would evoke the wrath of the gods. A marriage would be solemnised by a hammer, it even consecrated the funeral pyre of dead warriors.

Many small silver and other metal hammers have been found in graves. Some of these are tiny, only 2cm long. Over forty hammers have been exhumed and they date from the late tenth century and early eleventh. Most are from Denmark, southern Norway and south eastern Sweden. These hammers often have a loop on them to attach them to various items of clothing and could be seen as the pagan equivalent of the Christian cross. Like the Christian cross they vary, some are elaborately worked in silver, with finely etched eagles' heads with piercing eyes at the end. Others are plainer, made from iron and are a lot simpler in design. In Iceland a different type of hammer was found. This was at Foss in Hrunamannahreppur in the south west of the country. This hammer dates from the tenth century. What makes it strange is that it is a compound of a pagan hammer and a Christian cross, as if the two religions were together. Perhaps the wearer worshipped both.

Figure 19 - Thor

There is a parallel between Thor's hammer and the Hindu god Indra's thunderbolt Vajra. Indra was a god of the skies, rain and lightning like Thor and Jupiter. Like Thor his colour was red or golden and he rides a chariot although this was drawn by bay horses rather than goats. There are many similarities between Indra and Thor. Both battled with monsters, Indra slayed the dragon Vitra and Thor the Midgard serpent at Ragnarok, the end of the world. Both are warrior gods as well as that of the weather. Both come from a sky god and an earth goddess, Thor from Odin and Jord; Indra, from Dyeus the sky god and his consort the earth. Both also had red hair. Like Thor, Indra threw a hammer like object. This was a disc with a hole in the middle. It had a handle by which it was grasped and when thrown it rotated spitting lightning and fire, looking similar to a Catherine wheel. But here again is the same symbology of fire.

Another god associated with hammers is the Celtic Sucellus, meaning 'the good striker'. This was a Gaulish god usually shown with a long handled hammer. Another Celtic god associated with a hammer or club is The Dagda. This was the Irish Father of all the gods who had a magic club. With this weapon he could heal or harm. One end was used as a violent weapon, the other to remedy maladies. In the Breton lands they had a 'mell Benniget', meaning 'the holy mallet'. This was a hammer with a round head or just a round stone. Interestingly it was laid on the forehead of the dying to release their souls up to the nineteenth century, just as the earlier Mjollnir of Thor had hallowed the dead. This custom is echoed in the practice of the Dean of the Sacred College striking the forehead of the Pope with a hammer made of ivory or precious metal before proclaiming his death.

The second treasure that Thor had was a belt called Megin-gjord. When he wore this magical belt, his strength was doubled. His third treasure was a pair of iron gauntlets called Iarn-greiper. This was necessary as his hammer was often red hot and he needed the gloves to grip it firmly.

Thor was also the protector and hallower of the dead. Various inscriptions have been found on stones. On one at Glavendrup in Fyn, dating from 900-925 CE, is inscribed with the words 'pur uiki pasi runar', meaning, 'may Thor hallow these runes'. Another stone in Virring in Denmark, again carved in the tenth century bears the epitaph; 'pur uiki pisis kuml', meaning, 'may Thor hallow this memorial'.

Sometimes the message on the stones is just *'pur uiki'*, *'may Thor hallow'* and sometimes a symbol of a hammer is added. It appears this was similar to the Christian inscriptions on grave stones of *'may God help his soul'*. Thor was obviously thought of as a very sacred god.

Thor had two wives. The first was the giantess Jarnsaxa, meaning *'Iron Cutlass'* or *'Iron Stone'*. She bore him two children Magni meaning *'colossal might'* and Modi meaning *'fierce courage'*. There is a story showing the strength of the child Magni. This involved a fight between the strongest giant of all, Hrungnir and Thor, Hrungnir had got drunk in Asgard, the home of the gods and boasted that he would destroy both Asgard and Valhalla, killing all the gods and goddesses. Thor was very angry and brandishing his hammer challenged Hrungnir to a duel.

This worried the giants. What would happen if Thor killed the strongest of them? What would their chances be? So the giants built a giant figure of clay. This was massive, nine leagues high and three broad under his armpits. But this caused the giants a problem, for they could not find a heart big enough for him. So they used a mare's. Hrungnir's heart was itself impressive. It was made of hard stone and sharp edged. But the clay giant called Mist Calf's heart was not up to it. Mist Calf was terrified, as Snorri said: *"it made water when it saw Thor".*[116]

Thor went to the duelling field with his follower Thjalfi. Thjalfi told Hrungnir to put down his shield which he had in front of him for Thor would attack him from below. So the giant placed his shield on the floor and stood on it. He held a whetstone to defend himself against Thor. Now Thor attacked. There was thunder and lightning. Thor threw his hammer. The hammer and whetstone met in mid air. The hammer smashed the giant's skull, but the whetstone was also damaged. It split in two and half of it lodged itself in Thor's head. The giant fell, but in doing so he trapped Thor, for he fell with his leg over the god's neck. No one could move him, all the gods tried. But the three year old Magni came and flung Hrungnir's leg of his father Thor', saying: *"What a pity I didn't come along sooner, father; I reckon I'd have struck the giant dead with my bare fist if I had met him."*[117] There was a son fit for the god of storms, Thor. Thor rewarded him with Hrungnir's horse Gold-mane.

---

[116] The Prose Edda of Snorri Sturluson, Young, 1964:104
[117] Ibid, 1964:105.

Figure 20 - Sif

Thor went home to Thrudvangar still with the bone in his head. But the sibyl called Groa, wife of Aurvandil the Brave, recited spells over him. This worked, the stone fell loose. Thor, pleased told how he had carried Aurvandil on his back in a basket with just his toes poking out. Unfortunately this toe froze and broke off. Thor hurled it into the sky where it became known as Aurvandil's toe. There was during this period a constellation by this name, although we don't know which star it was. Evidently Groa was so pleased that she stopped evoking her spell. Because of this the stone was never fully removed from Thor's head.

Thor's other wife was Sif, a prophetess and fertility goddess with long golden hair, a very beautiful woman. Thor was very proud of his wife's magnificent golden hair. Sif symbolised the earth, and her hair represented the long grass or the golden grain covering the harvest fields. One morning she awoke and her hair had gone, she had been shorn while she slept by the mischievous Loki. Thor was enraged. He took his hammer and went to find Loki. Loki changed shape to try and hide from the angry god, but to no avail. Thor caught the errant god and almost strangled him in his rage. Loki had to agree to procure for poor Sif a new head of hair, as good as the old.

Loki went down to the bowels of the earth to plead with the dwarf Dvalin. Dvalin fashioned the finest gold thread, this when touching Sif's head would grow into a new head of hair. The dwarf also made the magical spear Gungnir which never failed in its aim and was given to Odin, and Freyr was given the ship Skidbladnir which travelled on air as well as water, always to the prevailing wind. The magical arm ring Draupnir and a golden-bristled boar were also made by the dwarf. Sif and Thor had a son called Loridi, who looked like his father.

Thor himself was a very popular god in the *Landnamabok*, the '*Book of Settlements*', a detailed history of Iceland from the thirteenth and later centuries; although it is likely that it dates back much further as there is evidence of this. Of some 260 settlements named in the document over a quarter bore names beginning with Thor. There were about 4000 people named in the book and of these nearly 1000 bore named starting with Thor. Very few of the other gods appear in people's names in this manner.

There are many stories demonstrating that for a while the two religions of paganism and Christianity run side by side, with Christians evoking Christ and pagans Thor. One of these concerns a man called Orlyg who was brought up in the Hebrides by *'the holy Bishop Patrick.'* This was St Patrick who died in 463 CE, and brought the Christian religion to Ireland and is patron saint of that land. Orlyg set sail for Iceland and was given a sacred bell and timbers by the bishop to build a church dedicated to St Columba (Kolumbilli). He went in one ship and his foster-brother Koll, in another. Both ships ran into a severe storm and got lost. Orlyg called on Patrick to assist him, but his foster-brother evoked the god Thor. Orlyg's ship arrived safely in a bay now called Patrick's Fjord (Patreksfjordr). His foster-brother was not so lucky, his ship was wrecked.

Another story demonstrates this rivalry. When Thorfinn Karlsefni and his retinue were exploring the New World, which they called Vinland, in the end of the tenth century, they became short of food. They were converted to Christianity and they prayed to Christ to help them. But one member of the party, Thorhall the Hunter was still of the older faith. He beseeched Thor for assistance. Here is the Saga called *Eirik's Saga*, I have reproduced it in full as it gives a good insight into the two contrasting faiths of that period:

> *"They stayed there that winter, which turned out to be a very severe one; they had made no provision for it during the summer, and now they ran short of food and the hunting failed. They moved out to the island in the hope of finding game or stranded whales, but there was little food to be found there, although their livestock throve. Then they prayed to God to send them something to eat, but the response was not as prompt as they would have liked.*
>
> *Meanwhile Thorhall the Hunter disappeared and they went out to search for him. They searched for three day; and on the fourth day Karlsefni and Bjarnin found him top of a cliff. He was staring up at the sky with eyes and mouth and nostrils agape, scratching himself and pinching himself and mumbling. They asked him what he was doing there; he replied that it was no concern of theirs, and told them not to be surprised and that he was old enough not to need them to look after him. They urged him to come back home with them, and he did.*

A little later a whale was washed up and they rushed to cut it up. No one recognised what kind of whale it was, not even Karlsefni, who was an expert on whales. The cooks boiled the meat, but when it was eaten it made them all ill.

Then Thorhall the Hunter walked over and said, "Has not Redbeard (this was the common name for Thor) turned out to be more successful than your Christ? This was my reward for the poem I composed in honour of my patron, Thor; he has seldom failed me."

When the others realised this they refused to use the whalemeat and threw it over a cliff, and committed themselves to God's mercy. Then a break came in the weather to allow them to go our fishing, and after that there was no scarcity of provisions."[118]

There appears to be a dispute between Christianity and Thor in the saga. It shows that Christianity was gaining the upper hand, for the meat was jettisoned when it was found that it had been provided by a heathen god.

Christian missionaries were sent to Iceland to stamp out the old religion. Thangbrand, a missionary from Germany went to the country, he found some powerful supporters of the new faith. But, not surprisingly, he was very unpopular with the ancient poets.

They made verses slandering him and his religion. He was called the *'effeminate enemy of the gods'* (*argan godvarg*). By now there was definite animosity between the two sides. One of the poets, Vetrlidi, especially vocal against the Christians, was murdered while he was cutting peat. Some of these poets such as the poetess, Steinunn, were very vocal and wrote many verses supporting Thor and the Norse gods. The missionaries murdered other poets who were spreading the heathen faith.

The rivalry between Thangbrand and Steinunn continued. Thangbrand's ship was driven on to a rock and severely damaged. Steinunn claimed a victory for Thor and the old gods. In the poetic verse of the time she described *'the keeper of the bell,'* the priest, whose ship had been destroyed. She said that the gods had driven this *'horse of*

---

[118] The Vinland Sagas, the Norse Discovery of America, Magnusson (trans) 1968:96.

Figure 21 - Longship

the sea', by which she meant ship, to be wrecked and the Christian Christ had not been able to protect it. To the Norse this was a bad omen as they expected the gods to protect them.

Steinunn now met her rival Thangbrand. The poetess tried to convert the missionary back into the old faith, but met with little success. She said that Thor had challenged Christ to a duel, but Christ had not dared to fight such a powerful god. Thangbrand replied that Thor would be nothing but dust and ashes, were it not God's will that he should survive.

In Norway too there was rivalry between the two faiths. There is the story of the meeting between Thor and Olaf Tryggvason, King of Norway. When the king was in his splendid ship called the Long Serpent, a handsome man with a red beard asked for passage. This was granted. He was knowledgeable in ancient history. He told the King and his crew about the land in which they were passing. The land had been peopled with giants who had died except for two old women. These giantesses persecuted the people who called on Thor to protect them. He appeared and brandishing his hammer slew the evil giantesses. Peace was restored. After finishing his tale, Thor dived into the sea and disappeared.

There is another story illustrating Christianity overcoming the earlier Heathenism. Here Jarl Eirik, the son of Hakon the Great defeated the king Olaf Tryggvason in the battle of Svold. Eirik until this point had been a Pagan but he swore that if he beat the king he would convert to the new religion. True to his word, on victory he replaced the image of Thor on his ship's prow with a cross.

Again in Sweden and Denmark there is the same story of rivalry between the two faiths, with Christianity winning over the older religion. In approx. 1030 CE an English missionary called Wilfred, publicly insulted and blasphemed an idol of Thor. He then smashed it to pieces with a double headed axe called a bipennis.

This was a battle between faiths. There could only be one outcome. The Scandinavian countries converted to the newer faith of Christianity.

Thor was also common in Ireland. There he was known as Tomair or Tomar. The Norse rulers of Dublin were called the tribe of Tomar, or *'muinter Tomair'*. There was also a *'Coill Tomair'* or Grove of Thor. This consisted of stately oaks and other large trees but was burned down by Brian Boru, King of Ireland from 976 CE, in around the year 1000 CE.

Thor was known in England as the god Thunor, meaning *'thunder'*, a very ancient deity. He was a weather god and controlled the heavens. He was one of the main Saxon gods as is shown in this nine century baptismal vow:

> *"I renounce all the words and works of the devil, Thunaer, Woden and Saxnot, and the demons who are their companions."*[119]

Thunaer is Thor, Woden is Odin and it is likely that Saxnot is the sword god, Tyr.

Thor was a common god in Britain, Germany and the Scandinavian world; he appears to have been one of the last Pagan gods to be worshipped before Christianity conquered the world.

---

[119] Myth and Religion of the North, Turnville-Petre, 1975:100.

FRIDAY

Friday is the sixth day of the week. To the Romans it was *Dies Veneris*, the *'day of Venus'*. Venus was the Roman goddess of love. In France the day is still named Vendredi, after the goddess. Venus is associated with the Germanic and Norse goddess of love, Frigg. Friday became Frigg's Day, or Frjadagr in Old Norse, and Friday. Frigg is also a goddess of love and was thought to have rather lose morals. There is a piece of verse in *Solomon and Saturn* that illustrates the connection between the two goddesses:

> *"The sixth day they appointed*
> *to the shameless goddess*
> *called Venus*
> *and Fricg (Frigg) in Danish."*[120]

Snorri in the *Edda* describes Frigg as Odin's wife and mother of the gods:

> *"His (Odin's) wife, the daughter of Fjorgvin, was named Frigg, and from that family has come the kindred that inhabited ancient Asgard and those kingdoms belonging to it: we call the members of that family the Aesir and they are all divinities."*[121]

Actually Frigg's parentage is quite confused. As well as being the daughter of Fjorgvin and Jord's sister, she is in some of the Sagas said to be the daughter of Jord, the earth goddess and Odin. Although they all seem to agree that she was the great god Odin's wife. As such at a Norse wedding her health was drunk together with that of Thor and Odin. She was an important goddess and could sit on the throne of Hlidskialf, alongside her husband Odin.

Frigg was the goddess of the atmosphere. She controlled the clouds. Because of this she usually wore either snow white or dark clothes to symbolise the clouds. She was

---

[120] The Vikings in England: Settlement, Society and Culture, Hadley, 2006:94.
[121] The Prose Edda of Snorri Sturluson, Young, 1964:37.

always richly dressed and loved jewels. She was a tall beautiful woman, usually depicted crowned with heron plumes symbolising silence. For once Frigg was told a secret, she would never reveal it. Around her waist was a golden girdle with a bunch of keys, the symbol of the Norse housewife, whom she represented in the hierarchy of Northern deities.

Snorri says that Frigg is the foremost of the goddesses. She lives in a magnificent palace called Fensalir, the *'hall of mists'*, marshes, or of the sea, in Asgard. It was from here that spins from an opulent jewelled spinning wheel. She would spin golden thread or brilliant coloured clouds. The wondrous cloud formations of the sky were created by this goddess. This spinning wheel could be seen in one of the constellations in the sky called in the North, Frigg's Spinning Wheel, and in the South Orion's Girdle.

Frigg could foretell the future, but never divulged what she saw. She was the goddess of marriage and motherly love. Although strangely for a goddess of marriage, she was not faithful. She had an affair with Odin's brothers Vili and Ve. But perhaps as a fertility goddess she was expected to be sexual. Certainly she had loose morals. Interestingly one common vulgarism coming from this goddess is the word *frig*, meaning to commit the sexual act.

Frigg had a magical feather coat, made from falcon skin. This enchanted coat gave her the power to fly like a bird and she could hover in the sky and visit all the Norse nine worlds.

Frigg was Queen of the gods, as such she had goddesses that attended her. One of these was Fulla, a beautiful virgin with long loose golden hair. She wore a gold band round her head. The golden hair symbolised golden grain and the golden band the binding of the sheaf. In Germany where this goddess was known as Abundia or Abundantia she was an earth goddess and portrayed the fruitfulness of the soil. She acted as a messenger for Frigg and was entrusted with the care of her jewel box and shoes. She was also privy to all her mistress' secrets and her general advisor.

The goddess Hlin was another attendant of Frigg's. Hlin was the goddess of consolation. A very attractive goddess she would kiss away the tears of the bereaved. She gave relief from the grief felt when loved ones passed away, listening to the mourners prayers with compassion. These pleas she carried to her mistress, Frigg with recommendations for assistance to those in the pain of loss of a loved one. Hlin also protects those men that Frigg wants to save from dangers.

Gna was Frigg's messenger. She had a miraculous horse called Hofvarpnir meaning 'Hoof flourisher'. This beast could fly rapidly through the air and over the sea. It symbolised the cool, refreshing breeze. Riding this swift mystical steed, Gna viewed all that occurred on the earth. She would report back to Frigg, everything she saw. Frigg was certainly a well informed goddess, as befits her position as the queen of the gods.

There is a lovely story concerning Gna. As she was passing over Hunaland, the land of the Huns, Gna saw King Rerir, a mortal who was descended from Odin; in fact Snorri says that he was Odin's grandson, being the son and heir of Odin's third son Sigi. Anyway Rerir was very unhappy. He and his queen were childless and he wanted a son to inherit his throne. Gna reported back to Frigg. Frigg was the goddess of childbirth and she took pity on the king. Taking a magical apple she gave it to Gna to take to Rerir. Gna dropped the apple into the surprised king's lap. Apples are a fertility symbol. Rerir gave it to his wife to eat. Nine months later their son, Volsung, was born. Volsung became king of the Huns after the death of his father and was himself a great Northern hero.

Here is a description of Gna on her fabulous beast here called Hoof-flinger from *Asgard and the Gods*:

> "'What flies up there, so quickly driving past?'
> Her answer from the clouds, as rushing by:
> 'I fly not, nor do drive, but harry fast,
> Hoof-flinger swift through cloud and mist and sky'"[122]

Snorri says that the Old Norse name meaning 'towering', for what soars high was derived from the goddess Gna.

---

[122] The Norsemen (Myths and Legends), Guerber, 1994:48.

Figure 22 – Frigg

Another of Frigg's attendants was the goddess, Lofn. Lofn was a gentle deity. She smoothed the way for lovers and helped couples for whom marriage was forbidden or banned. Snorri says that from her came the Old Norse word for *'permission'*.

Yet another attendant of the Queen of the gods was Vjofn. This was the goddess of peace and conciliation. She reconciled quarrelling couples. This goddess was called Sjofn in Norse and the Old Norse word *sjafni* meaning *'love'* comes from her name.

The goddess Syn had control over the door of Frigg's palace. She guarded the entrance, refusing to allow anyone not authorised to enter. Once Syn had decided you could not set foot in Frigg's hall, she would not change her mind, you were definitely barred. She presided over all tribunals and trials. When anyone denied an accusation it was said: *"Syn is brought forward"*. Syn's name meant *'denial'* or *'truth'*.

There was also Eira, the goddess of medicine, who served Frigg, queen of gods. She was said to heal wounds and diseases. In the Norse tradition only women practised medicine. This was highly unusual in ancient traditions as the world of medicine in other cultures was usually male.

Another of Frigg's attendants was the goddess Vara. This was the goddess of oaths. All pledges were heard by her. The keeping of oaths was very important indeed to the Norse. Any breaking of your word was harshly punished by Vara, she took vengeance. But if the pledges were kept, especially in difficult conditions, this goddess would reward the oath taker. Oaths in Old Norse were called *vdrar*, meaning *'promises'* after this goddess.

There was the wise goddess Vor. She also served Frigg. Nothing could be hidden from her, she knew everything that was to happen in the world. Vor means *'faith'*.

Yet another of Frigg's servants was the goddess Snotra. She was wise and gentle and the goddess of virtue. When a man or women was self controlled they were called *snotr* after this goddess meaning *'prudent'*.

Another of Frigg's attendants was called Gefjon. She was a virgin goddess. Unmarried and chaste women were in her care. When these maidens die they are received by this goddess and made happy.

There is a lovely story about Gefjon. She did not remain a virgin but slept with King Gylfi, king of Sweden. The king only saw a beggar woman and did not realise that Gefjon was one of the Aesir, a goddess. As a reward for the pleasure she had given him he allowed her as much land as she could plough in a day and a night. Gefjon had four sons by a giant. These she turned into oxen and yoked them to the plough. Gefjon worked the oxen hard, sweat poured from them. She managed to plough a furrow so deep and wide that the king was amazed. She worked a massive amount of land. The land that she had ploughed was pulled into the sea and dragged into Denmark, where the goddess named it Zealand. This left a large crater which filled with water and became first Logrum, the sea and then Lake Malaren. This made Denmark larger and Sweden smaller. It is said to be the reason why Zealand is exactly the same the same shape as Malaren. All the indentations of the headlands of Zealand are supposed to be the same as those of the lake like a jigsaw.

Here is Snorri describing the event in the *Edda*:

"Gefjon dragged with laughter
from Gylfi liberal prince
what made Denmark larger,
so that beasts of draught
the oxen reeked with sweat;
four heads they had, eight eyes to boot
who went before broad island-pasture
ripped away as loot."[123]

Gefjon then married one of Odin's sons Scyld. She became the founders of the royal Danish race of Scyldings which dwelt in the city of Leire, in Denmark, the city she founded. This became a sacred city and many sacrifices were held there. The Danes are referred to as Scyldings in many Norse myths.

The references to Gefjon and ploughing are clearly fertility symbols. Ploughing the soil symbolises the marriage of the Earth and Heaven. Evidently the words *langala* (plough) and *lingam* both derive from a root-word denoting

---

[123] The Prose Edda of Snorri Sturluson, Young, 1964:29.

both the spade and the phallus. In the *Penguin Dictionary of Symbols*, this association is made clearer:

> "Like most cutting implements, spades and ploughs symbolise the action of the male principle upon passive, and therefore female, matter. The plough share symbolises the penis which penetrates the soil with is analogous to the female sexual organ."[124]

But back to the plough itself. There is a connection between this ancient story of Gefjon and some rituals involving the plough. In North West Europe a token strip of land is often ploughed at the beginning of spring, before the sowing of crops in the fields, to ensure fertility. There is also mentioned in Sir James Frazer's *The Golden Bough*, a ploughing ceremony in the Prussian area of Germany held in the spring. This consists of the ploughmen and sowers being splashed with water when they returned home by the farmer's wife and servants. The farmer's wife might claim exemption of the next part of the ritual by paying a forfeit but everyone else was ducked into a pond and submerged under water. This strange rite involves both ploughs and water, both of which were featured in the tale about Gefjon and Gylfi.

In England there are the remains of a holiday associated with the plough, this is Plough Monday on the first Monday after Twelfth Day, January 6th. This was considered the time after the festivities of the Christmas season that the Spring ploughing commenced. In Tusser's *Five Hundred Points of Good Husbandry*, written in 1573 CE are the following verses describing the festival:

> "Plough Monday, next after that twelfth-tide is past,
> Bids out with the Plough; the worst husband is last:
> If Ploughman get hatchet, or whip to the Skrene,
> Maids lose their cock, no water to be seen:"[125]

This strange verse is explained in Hilman's *Tusser Redivivus*, of 1710 CE:

> "After Christmas (which formally, during the twelve days, was a time of very little work) every gentleman

---

[124] The Penguin Dictionary of Symbols, Chevalier & Gheerbrant, 1996.
[125] Five Hundred Points of Good Husbandry, Tusser, 1984:270.

feasted the farmers, and every farmer their servants and task men. Plough Monday puts them in the mind of their business. In the morning the men and the maid servants strive who shall show their diligence in rising earliest. If the ploughman can get his whip, his plough-staff, hatchet, or anything that he wants in the field, by the fire-side, before the maid hath got her kettle on, then the maid loseth her Shrove tide cock, and it wholly belongs to the men. Thus did our forefathers strive to allure yours to their duty, and provided them innocent mirth as well as labour."[126]

This festival gradually altered through the years becoming a time when the plough was drawn through the village and farm labourers would solicit *'plough money'* from the villagers. If this was not given the land in front of the relevant house was ploughed. Though more often the money was freely given and the labourers danced round the plough. The plough was called the Fool Plough or White Plough. This was a time of mummers all dressed in white bedecked with vividly coloured ribbons and flowers. There were also in some areas sword dancing. A man would dress up in women's clothes. He was called the Bessy and would carry a collection box. It was a time of great gaiety.

In the church there was a Plough Sunday service, which still occurs in some rural communities today. The plough is actually bought into the church. Prayers are said for a good harvest and the plough is blessed.

Frigg was obviously a very important deity with so many attendants serving her needs. But strangely there is little left to know about how she was worshipped. No temples or shrines have been found dedicated to her. Little is now known about this eminent goddess. Like so many other ancient traditions the worship of Frigg, the goddess of love, has disappeared into thin air.

Frigg is often confused with the goddess Freya, goddess of beauty, sex and love. They share some of the same responsibilities and characteristics. Freya was identified with Frigg in Germany while in Norway, Sweden, Denmark and Iceland they appear to have separate identities.

---

[126] Dictionary of Faiths and Folklore, Hazlitt, 1995:495.

Freya was also something of a war goddess. She would ride into battle and chose one half of the slain, leaving the other for Odin. This is reflected in the name of her home in Asgard, Folkvangar, meaning *'Field of Warriors'*. Here she had her large and roomy palace called Sessrumnir, meaning *'With many seats'*. Her position on the battle field is shown by usually being depicted carrying a helmet, shield and spear. Here is Snorri's description of her in the *Edda*:

> *"Folkvangar's where*
> *Freyja (Freya) decides*
> *who shall sit where in the hall;*
> *half the slain every day*
> *she chooses*
> *and Odin has half."*[127]

It was at Folkvangar where Freya would entertain women so that they could still enjoy the company of their fallen lovers or husbands. So enticing was this prospect that many Northern woman would rush up to the battle field and fall upon swords or chose be burned with their spouses on the funeral pyre so that they could meet again under the care of this loving goddess.

Snorri describes her as the most renowned of the goddesses. He says that she is easily evoked and excellent to call on for help in love affairs. Love songs would be evoked in Freya's honour. Her name in German is used as we would use the verb *'to woo'*, so powerful was Freya. When Freya wept she cried tears of red gold. Evidently this goddess adores love poetry as befitting a goddess of love. It is from Freya that the Germans call married women Far.

Freya itself means *'lady'* as her twin brother, the god Freyr, means *'lord'*. This is interesting as the Greek god of fertility, Adonis, also means *'lord'*. Baal the Egyptian god of vegetation again means *'lord'*. Again the Babylonian and Assyrian god Tammuz, another agricultural deity, was also known as Adonis, meaning *'lord'*. Evidently many gods and goddess in many civilisations were referred to by these titles.

Freya was said to ride in a chariot pulled by two cats. This is echoed in the Phrygian goddess Kybele. Phrygia is in modern north-western Turkey. Kybele is a Mother goddess.

---

[127] The Prose Edda of Snorri Sturluson, Young, 1964:53.

Figure 23 - Freya

Like Freya she drove a chariot driven by lions or panthers, which are of the family of cats. Kybele is a very ancient goddess dating back to at least 1500 BCE. She was known as Cybele to the Romans who also worshipped her.

Tacitus describes a Germanic fertility and earth goddess called Nerthus. She is very similar to the northern deities of Frigg and Freya. Tacitus says that there was a sacred chariot drawn by two cows in which an image of the goddess Nerthus was carried. So holy was this chariot that it was taboo to all but priests of Nerthus who escorted the procession. As the carriage passed people honoured the goddess by ceasing warfare and laying down their arms. After the goddess was carried around the local area the vehicle and idol were returned to a secret lake, thought to be the Schwartze See, in Rugen, in the north of Germany, where they were washed and stored ready for use again. Those slaves attending to this ceremony were drowned in the lake.

Ornate chariots that would have been used for these ceremonies have been found by archaeologists in Dejbjerg, near Ringkjobing in Jutland. It dates from the early Iron Age. Another elaborate chariot was found in the Oseberg grave. This grave dates from the nine century. It was the custom then to be buried with your worldly goods. Chariots symbolised death, fertility and rebirth.

Both Freya and her brother Freyr are associated with a golden boar called Gullinbursti, meaning *'golden bristled'*, and Hildisvin, meaning *'battle boar'*. Gullinbursti a special wild boar had been made by a dwarf called Brock. Freya herself had a nickname of Syr meaning *'sow'*. Her other names are Mardoll, *'Horn'*, Vanadis, goddess of the Vanas, and Gefn, the latter meaning *'giver'*. This magical boar was capable of galloping through the air and the sea faster than any horse. It also had glowing bristles which allowed the gods and goddesses riding it to see in the night. The boar is another fertility symbol.

Freya like Frigg possessed a magical coat made from falcons. With this feathered coat on she could fly where she wished in the world. Freya had a necklace called Brisingamen, the Necklace of the Brisings. It had been fashioned by four dwarves. An exquisite piece of work and

Freya wanted it. But she had to sleep with the dwarves to receive it. Once she had it thought the goddess always wore it day and night.

Freya was lusted after by the gods. She appears to have slept with many of them. In fact the god Loki said that she had been loved and wedded by all the gods in turn. Among the gods she married were Odin symbolising the sky, her brother Freyr symbolising the fruitful rain, and Odur symbolising the sunshine. She was a sexy goddess.

Freya was said to have taught the gods witchcraft. But that could have been introduced after the ancient pagan religions were subsumed into the newer Christianity. Certainly the worship of Freya was demonized. Even today witches are associated with black cats, something that dates back to Freya who used to be depicted with cats. Toasts that were drunk in her honour were transferred to the Virgin Mary or St. Gertrude, a Frankish saint who died in 664 CE and was the patron saint of travellers. Thus another heathen deity was Christianised and disappeared into mythology.

SATURDAY

Saturday derives from the Latin *Saturni dies*, day of Saturn. Saturn was the Roman god of agriculture. The Latin root of the name is *sat*, meaning *'abundance'* and *satum* meaning *'sown'*, both very relevant to farming and cultivation. Saturn is also associated with the Greek god Cronos, god of time, perhaps better known as Old Father Time, an old man with a mantle thrown over his head. In his hand he holds a sickle. Even today time is often presented by this symbolism. Time was thought of as eternally young, now as ever old.

To the Norse Saturday, the last day of the week, was known as Laugardag, or *'wash day'*. It was a day sacred to Loki. Loki was a god of the hearth fire and the spirit of life. But he became the *'wizard of lies'*, the exact counterpart of the mediaeval Christian Lucifer, a god and devil combined. Saturday owes its name to Sataere, the thief in ambush and an agricultural god as well as the classical and perhaps better known god Saturn. Sataere is another name for the god Loki.

Loki is a strange god. He was a trickster, a mischief maker. Snorri in the *Edda* gives this rather unflattering portrait of him:

> *"Also reckoned amongst the gods is one that some call the mischiefmonger of the Aesir and the father-of-lies and the disgrace-of-gods-and-men. He is the son of the giant Farbauti and his name is Loki or Lopt. His mother's name is Laufey or Nal, and Byleist and Helblindi are his brothers. Loki is handsome and fair of face, but has an evil disposition and is very changeable of mood. He excelled all men in the art of cunning, and he always cheats. He was continually involving the Aesir in great difficulties and he often helped them out again by guile. His wife's name is Sigyn; their son Nari or Narvi."*[128]

---

[128] The Prose Edda of Snorri Sturluson, Young, 1964:55.

His name is interesting. The meaning of Loki is unknown, but it may come from the Proto-Indo-European *leuk-* meaning *'light'*[129] and cognate with the Latin *lux* which forms part of Lucifer, meaning *'the light bearer'*. Loki was the god of the destructive fire, which devastates. This could be where the later Christian Devil or Lucifer got associated with flames and the fires of Hell.

This theme of ravishing fire is emphasised in Loki's parents names. His father Farbauti's name means *'Dangerous Smiter'* and his mother Laufey's name could mean *'tree'* or *'leafy island'*. Loki is a union of the two, as are his brothers Byleist meaning the *'Trampler of Towns'* or *'Whirlwind from the east'*, and Helblindi meaning *'Helblinder'* or perhaps *'water spout'*. All these are strong forces. Branston in *Gods of the North*, argues that this suggests that Farbauti was a thunder storm giant whose children were the whirlwind and the water spout. Loki was therefore a destructive forest fire born from the lightning and the tree. Forest fires were then as now dreadful natural disasters, greatly feared.

Loki's relationship with the other gods appears blurred. He seems to have gone through a blood brother ceremony with Odin. Here is *Seamund's Edda*:

> *"Odin! Dost thou remember*
> *When we in early days*
> *Blended our blood together?*
> *When to taste beer*
> *Thou did'st constantly refuse*
> *Unless to both 'twas offered?"*[130]

Loki was first married to Glut, meaning *'glow'*. Together they had two daughters Eisa meaning *'embers'*, and Einmyria meaning *'ashes'*. As Loki means fire his family seem to represent the hearth fire. Interestingly there is an old folktale in the North which relates that when the flames were crackling in the hearth it was said that was Loki beating his children.

---

[129] See Dictionnaire Etymologique du Proto-Indo-Européen, Carnoy, 1955:51.
[130] The Norsemen (Myths and Legends), Guerber, 1994:162.

Loki also married the giantess Angrboda. The couple had three children all monsters, Hel, the goddess of death, Jormungand, the Midgard serpent and Fenrir the fiend wolf.

Loki's third wife was Sigyn, who was a loyal and faithful wife. Sigyn stood by Loki even after he had been thrown out of Asgard by the other gods. They had two mortal sons Narve and Vali. Vali later killed his brother Narve.

Loki was a strange character. In the *Edda* it is related that Loki was mother of Odin's mystical eight legged horse Sleipnir, the father being the stallion Svadilfari. Here is the relevant passage in the *Edda*: *"Loki however, had had such dealings with Svadilfari that time later he bore a foal."* It is quite clear that the god is here bisexual.

Loki's sexuality is referred to in the *Short Voluspa* which says he ate the half roasted heart of an evil woman. From eating this organ he became pregnant. Again he is both male and female. The *Short Voluspa* is an Icelandic verse which was preserved in the late fourteenth century work known as the *Flateyjarbok*. It is a useful source of extra information of this period.

This is echoed in the poem *Lokasenna*, meaning 'the flight of Loki'. In this verse Loki is described by Odin:

> *"You were seven years below the earth,*
> *milking cows as a woman;*
> *you have borne children*
> *and I thought that the way of a 'paederast.'"*[131]

Here again is the reference to Loki giving birth to children. Loki was a shape changer, this is evident in many of the myths. It also appears that he was also a sex changer. Bisexuality was frowned upon by the Norse. It was considered unmanly, an *ergi*, a term of insult. In fact according to the Icelandic law there were three very insulting words which all meant homosexuality. They were *ragr*, *strodinn*, and *sordinn*. Homosexuals were made outlaws by the law.

Loki was sly, devious and a liar. He caused many problems for the gods. But perhaps his worse crime was to cause the death of the god Baldur, also called Baldr, by his brother Hodur, sometimes called Hoder or Hod. Baldur was

---

[131] Myth and Religion of the North, Turnville-Petre, 1975:130.

a kind, gentle god. It was the mischievous Loki who precipitated his death by tricking his blind brother Hodur into throwing a shaft of mistletoe and killing him

The gods are devastated by Baldur's death. Aegir the god of the sea, invites the gods, to a feast in his coral caves in the bottom of the sea. Here is it described in the *Valhalla*:

> *"Now to assuage the high gods' grief*
> *And bring their mourning some relief,*
> *From the coral caves*
> *`Neath ocean waves,*
> *Mighty King Aegir*
> *Invited the Aesir*
> *To Festival*
> *In Hlesey's hall;*
> *That, tho' for Baldur every guest*
> *Was grieving yet,*
> *He might forget*
> *Awhile his woe in friendly teast."*[132]

All the gods arrived in the cave, even Loki who was not invited. But even here this errant god called trouble. Aegir's home was a sanctuary, no violence was allowed. But Loki got jealous when the other gods praised Aegir's servant, Funfeng, for his excellence at waiting upon his master's guests. Loki killed one of them. For this he was banned from the cave.

The evening started. Loki crept back in and sat with the other gods. He started to hurl abuse, taunting them. Here Loki's clever tongue stood him in good stead, for all his insults had a ring of truth around them. He pointed out all the gods various weaknesses. This particular verse shows that the Norse gods all had faults.

Odin was said to have given victories to cowards instead of brave warriors. He was also sited to have dabbled in witchcraft. The other gods fared no better. The goddess Freya, Loki taunted about her lovers saying that she had slept with all the gods and elves and even her own brother. Thor got very angry and brandished his hammer, the mighty Mjollnir at the wayward deity. At this Loki fled.

---

[132] The Norsemen (Myths and Legends), Guerber, 1994:167.

Figure 24 - Loki

Enough was enough. The gods decided to do something about the troublesome Loki. Loki meanwhile had escaped to a mountain hideout. Here he built a house with four doors so that he could see in every direction. During the day Loki, changed into a salmon and hid in a waterfall called Franang.

Loki became scared that the Aesir would catch him. He could evade a hook, but what if the gods used a net? That would be more difficult. The more he thought about the net the more worried he became. What sort of net would be used? A fishing net had never been made before. But still Loki worried, he got some cord and experimented, trying different types of mesh.

The all seeing Odin had discovered where he was hiding. Taking with him the gods Kvasir and Thor, Odin went to capture the devious Loki. Loki saw the danger, and threw the net he working on in the fire, instantly changing back into a salmon, swam to safety in the river.

The three gods found Loki's mountain hideaway. The hut was empty, but Kvasir saw the remains of the burnt net in the fire. This netting had never been used before, but Kvasir saw the importance of its use in catching fish. He reasoned that Loki was now in the form of a salmon and as such could be caught in the net. The gods sat down and took the charred remains of the netting to see how it was constructed. A duplicate was made, Loki's days were numbered.

The first time the gods cast the net, Loki swam and evaded it. The gods tried again, this time weighing the net. This time Loki as a salmon managed to leap upstream and again avoid the mesh. It was said that this was the first time that the salmon could jump. The third time the wayward god was not so lucky. The gods cast again. Loki was caught by Thor in mid leap. Thor had caught him by the tail. It is because of this that the salmon tapers towards the tail.

Loki was now caught. He had to be punished for his crimes. He was dragged away and incarcerated in a cave. Here he was bound, for not only must he be disciplined, he also must not be allowed to escape and continue with his transgressions. Loki's two sons, Vali, and Narfi were also captured. Vali was turned into a ferocious wolf and while in that form tore apart his brother Narfi. Narfi's entrails were taken from his body and used to bind his father Loki. Loki was bound to three flat stones; one under his shoulder, one under his loins, and the last under his knee joints. The entrails then became iron. There was no way that Loki could escape back to Asgard and cause trouble again, although he would be released at Ragnarok.

To add to Loki's torture, the giantess Skadi, placed a venomous snake over Loki's face. The venom of this snake, would drip, drop by drop over the god's upturned face until the end of the world Ragnarok brings relief and freedom. Loki was certainly punished, when the gods penalised they gave harsh punishment.

Loki's wife Sigyn, was faithful and devoted to her husband. She could have returned to Asgard, but chose to stay with Loki. The loyal Sigyn sat by him with a basin catching the venom before it fell over Loki's face. Only when Sigyn had to empty the bowl would the poison fall on her husband. Such was the love she had for her husband that she stayed with him, assisting him and saving him from pain until the day of the Ragnarok.

Loki was in agony. He would scream and shout in pain. He would try to break free from his chains. So great was the power that Loki used trying to escape from his fetters that the earth would shake. This became known as earthquakes.

Although Loki's crimes were great, his punishment seems very harsh. There is a parallel here with Christianity. By this time Loki appears to have become the equivalent of Satan. For the Antichrist will be bound in Hell, and only break free at the Day of Judgement, for the last battle of Armageddon. Armageddon is the counterpart of the Norse Ragnarok.

Figure 25 - The Norns

APPENDIX

PAGAN SAXON/NORSE FESTIVALS

Not a great deal survives about the calendar in Saxon days. The Venerable Bede left a rather sparse account of the pagan year in a section of the *De Temporum Ratione*.

Bede states that the pagan year began on December 25th. The longest night of the year, the winter solstice was called *'modra nect'*, or Mothers Night. This was even noted in an article in the *Gentleman's Magazine* of 1784 CE, which said that Mother's Night had been celebrated by our ancestors. The month started on the solstice and was dedicated to the gods Thor and Freyr. It was a time of feasting and merrymaking. It was called *Giuli* by Bede, but the exact meaning of this word is uncertain.

Bede called the second month of the year *Solmonath*. According to Bede this was when *"cakes were offered to the gods"*. This is strange as an explanation of the origin of the name because *sol* means *'sun'*. Now in the Norwegian calendar the month is called *Lios-beri*, meaning *'light bringing'*. The Norwegian and Saxons both worshipped the same gods, the religions being very similar; the meaning of the month also appears the same.

To the Norse this month was dedicated to the god Vali, the god of light. Vali was the son of Odin and Rind, the earth goddess. It fell between the middle of January and February. It is interesting that Vali as god of light is often depicted with arrows and a bow. This is a reference to arrows being symbolic of beams of light. Of course arrows are associated with love and this month falls on Valentine's Day, the day of lovers. The Christian saint, St. Valentine was often depicted with arrows. There appears to be a direct relationship with this early Christian saint and the pagan god Vali. Lios-beri was represented by the sign of the bow.

This association of the end of January and the beginning of February with light is reflected in the Christian festival of Candlemass Day on February 2nd. This is the feast of the purification of the Virgin Mary. In the Roman Catholic

Church part of this ceremony is a candle procession. Yet more light.

But back to Bede, Solmonath, and cakes. February was the start of the ploughing season. There is an old Anglo-Saxon charm which says that cakes were placed in the first furrow ploughed. This was a fertility rite to ensure an abundant harvest.

Bede said that the third and fourth months of the Old English year were named from two goddesses called Hretha and Eostre. Not much has survived about Hretha. Eostre was the Saxon goddess of Spring, sometimes known as Eastre or Ostara. It was this goddess that gave her name to the Christian feast of Easter. Eostre was a popular goddess and managed to escape the demonising which was the fate of many of the pagan deities. The egg, the beginning of life, an ancient fertility symbol attributed to the goddess was transferred to the Easter festival. In parts of Germany however there remains more tangible evidence of Eostre. There are stone altars known as Easter-stones. These altars are dedicated to the goddess Ostara. They were decorated with flowers. Despite the warning of priests dances were still held around the light of bonfires lit to commemorate the goddess. These popular festivities continued until the middle of the last century.

Bede named the fifth month *Thrimilci*. It had this name because it was the time that the cows were milked three times a day. That would have been correct for the farming year of May. It was also the period of the May Day festivals originally dedicated to the god Odin.

The sixth and seventh month were both called *Litha* according to Bede. Bede described this month as *"blandus sive navigabilis"*,[133] meaning *'calm weather for voyages'*. The weather would be mild at this time of the year. This period would include the summer solstice, the longest day in the year. After that the nights would grow longer.

Now the summer is coming to a head we have according to Bede the month of *Weodmonath* meaning the *'weed month'*. It is August that the weeds grow. It would have been a time of work for the rural Saxon.

---

[133] De Temporum Ratione, Bede.

September the month of the harvest is suitably named by Bede as *Halegmonath*, the *'holy month'* or *'month of offerings'*. It would be when devotions would be made to the goddess for fruitful and abundant harvests; a time of what is now known as Harvest festivals.

Now we are coming up to the autumn. Bede says that this month is called *Wintirfyllith*, the *'winter full moon'*. It was a time to prepare for the coming winter.

The month of November was called *Blotmonath*, meaning the *'blood month'*. This would have been a time when animals would have been sacrificed. They would have been offered to the gods, together with the plea for a kind winter to survive till the following spring when a new cycle would start.

The Norse had a god of winter, the harshest time of their year. He was called Ull. To the Anglo-Saxons this god was known as Vulder, but in the Germanic countries he was known as Uller, or Holler. The origin of the name is contested, including the gothic *wullpus*, means *'glory'*, or *'brilliance'*. The Old English version of his name is *wuldor*, meaning glory, *'splendour'*, or *'honour'*. Certainly as well as a god of winter, Ull was the god of hunting, archery, death and skiing.

Snorri in the *Edda* describes him as:

> *"He is such a good archer and ski-runner that no one can rival him. He is beautiful to look at as well and he has all the characteristics of a warrior. He is also good to call on him in duels."*[134]

The Norse originated from Iceland where the winter season was long and severe. There was a lot of snow. Ull wore snow shoes. Snow shoes were sometimes constructed from bone. It was said that he travelled on snow by bone, which could of course be an ancient form of ski. Snow shoes turned up in the front so as they resembled the prow of a ship. Perhaps it was this that became the story that Ull had chanted magical runes over his snow shoes changing them into an enchanted vessel. This ship would carry him over land or water. Some say he changed his shield into the boat. Snow shoes are also shaped as shields. Ull was therefore a

---

[134] The Prose Edda of Snorri Sturluson, Young, 1964:55.

god of shields and as such the deity to evoke for protection in a duel.

Ull was patron of the first month of the Norse year which began on November 22nd. This was the time when the sun came into the constellation of Sagittarius, the bowman. This is very apt as Ull was the god of archers and hunting. Ull was said to have lived in Ydalir the land of Yew dales. The finest bows for archery were made from yew so it is fitting that the god of archers would come from the land where this wood was plentiful.

Oaths were sworn on the sacred arm ring of Ull. So powerful was this ring, that if anyone lied while swearing this solemn oath, it would shrink and sever the dishonest person's hand. It would appear that Ull was associated with security and the law.

Ull had various temples dedicated to him. These were popular during the months of November and December. Folk would beseech Ull to lay a protective covering of snow on their lands.

Ull was responsible for illuminating the sky with the Aurora Borealis, those magnificent flashing lights that brighten the Northern sky. As Ull was the god of winter he was banished to Hel by Odin in the summer, to reappear again in the next winter.

When the Norse religion was Christianised Ull became St. Hubert, the hunter. Hubert who died in 727 CE, was the bishop of Maestricht and Liege. He was converted to Christianity after seeing an image of Christ between the antlers of a stag. There are doubts of the truth of this story and it was only popularised after the 14th century. In paintings Huber is depicted with a stag at his feet. His hunting horn is on view in the Wallace collection in London. There are links between this saint, the patron of hunting and huntsman, and Ull the god of hunting. He was another ancient deity who was changed into a more acceptable Christian form.

MAY DAY

May Day was a time to celebrate the end of the long winter and the beginning of the spring. These spring ceremonies were important both in this country and in other more northern lands where some of them originated from. The sixteenth century Swedish writer Olaus Magnus said:

> *"That after their long winter, from the beginning of October the end of April, the Northern nations have a custom to welcome the returning splendour of the sun with dancing, and mutually to feast each other, rejoicing that a better season for fishing and hunting was approached."*[135]

This theme continued in Northern countries. At May Day the Goths and Southern Swedes would engage in a mock battle between summer and winter. In Sweden there was a flower decked May king who battled with a fur decked Winter figure. The May King would throw blossom at Winter causing him to flee, for now spring was here. This was called the May Ride.

There was a similar ceremony in the Isle of Man. Here you had a contest between a floral clothed Queen of May and fur clad Queen of Winter. The Queen of Winter was a man who dressed in woman's clothes. Each of the two antagonists had followers who dressed in the appropriate clothes regarding the two seasons. And each team had their own captain.

George Waldron, in his *Description of the Isle of Man* in 1726 describes this fascinating custom great detail:

> *"both companies march till they meet on a common, and then their trains engage in a mock battle. If the Queen of Winter's forces get the better, so far as to take the Queen of May prisoner, she is ransomed, for as much as pays for the expenses of the day. After this ceremony Winter and her company retire, and divert themselves in a barn, and the others remain on the*

---

[135] Dictionary of Faiths and Folklore, Hazlitt, 1995:397.

green, where having danced a considerable time. They conclude the evening with a feast; the Queen at one table with her maids, the captain and his troops at another. There are seldom less than fifty or sixty people at each board..."[136]

Unfortunately this picturesque and important custom died out in the Isle of Man in the eighteenth century; yet another example of the loss of a meaningful ritual known to our ancestors.

The fashionable distinct of London the celebrated Mayfair, gets its name as being the site of a May fair. It was originally called Brookfield. The May Fair was held on the site of the present Hertford Street, Curzon Street, and Shepherd Market. This was an annual fair held during the reign of Edward I held on the eve of St. James whose Saint's day is on the 25th July. The fair then had the title of the St James Fair. This fair was suppressed in 1664 CE but reinstated by James II. The new fair was on May 1st and became the local May fair from which the area got its name.

The best known ritual of Mayday is that of the Maypole. Sometimes these poles were erected every year, others were more permanent. But even those longstanding poles did not endure for that long. Being made of wood the base would rot and the whole pole have to be replaced. The average life of a Maypole was only fifteen years.

Maypoles were tall. Welford-on-Avon had its own permanent pole. It was painted with red stripes and was seventy feet high. Another pole at Barwick-in-Element near Leeds was even taller. This massive pole was eighty or ninety feet high.

The London church of St Andrew Undershaft, in Leadenhall Street, lies beside a mayshaft, used at this important day. This maypole was erected every year. It was enormous. John Stow writing in 1598 CE in his *A Survey of London* comments on this remarkable pole:

"in the midst of the street before the south door of the said church; which shaft, when it was set on end and

---

[136] Dictionary of Faiths and Folklore, Hazlitt, 1995:387.

fixed in the ground, was higher than the church steeple."[137]

There was a maypole in the Strand erected during the reign of Elizabeth I on the site now occupied by the Church of St Mary-le-Strand. This was demolished by the Puritans, who destroyed so much of our old heritage, in 1644 CE. The pole was re-erected in 1661 CE; it is said by the farrier John Clarges who was celebrating his daughter's marriage to General Monk. This maypole was huge; it was 134 ft high (40.8m) and made of cedar. The maypoles on this site appear to have a chequered history. The 1661 CE pole perished was perished and needed a replacement in 1713 CE. This newer pole however was bought by the noted Sir Isaac Newton, where in 1718 CE he sent it to a friend in Wanstead. It was then erected in the park with a new purpose, to support the then largest telescope in Europe.

Dances were held round the Maypole. People would join hands and form a circle round the pole. Moving around the shaft clockwise they would sing and stamp their feet on the earth. The ritual chant would be sung to tune of what we would recognise as *Here We Go Round the Mulberry Bush.* Here are the words:

"Here we go round the merry Maypole
The merry Maypole, the merry Maypole,
Here we go round the merry Maypole
On a cold and frosty May morning!"[138]

Now the dancers would stop their encircling of the pole. For now it was time to enact the ritual of *'collecting the May'.* The May was a term describing the evergreen boughs and flowers collected at this time of the year before dawn by eager your men and women. This foliage would be shaped into wreaths and decorations which adorned rooms and the maypole itself. This early morning festive trip to the woodlands was called *'Going-a-Maying'.* The next part of the traditional May day song describes this ritual:

"This is the way we collect the May...
On a cold and frosty May morning."[139]

---

[137] A Survey of London, Stow, 2007:163.
[138] Medieval Holidays and Festivals, Cosman, 1984:54.

The dancers would bend down to illustrate the picking of meadow flowers and reach up to illustrate the gathering of the branches for the May.

The next part of the ritual interprets the May rite of May Dew. The dew of a May morning was collected. It was considered lucky. The water was healing and was said to be able to cure such ailments as consumption, goitre, spinal weakness, and poor sight. It was also rubbed into the skin to create a wonderful complexion. The lines in the song went:

"This is the way we gather the May dew...
On a cold and frosty May morning"[140]

The next part of the chant is about stamping the earth. Each dancer would lift their right knee high in the air. The foot would be stamped down into the ground hard, again and again. The chant went:

"This is the way we stamp for Spring...
On a cold and frosty May morning"[141]

The next verse describes Jack-in-the-Green. Here associated with the baking of gingerbread men. Jack-in-the-Green is also known a representative of Summer, the bringer-in of a time of plenty. He takes the form of a young man totally encased in a wickerwork cage. This cage is smothered in green branches, leaves and flowers. The only parts of him visible are his feet and his eyes poking out from his green cage. Jack-in-the-Green is part of the traditional Mayday procession. Interestingly this ancient figure became to be associated with chimney sweeps. In the latter half of the eighteenth century, sweeps took over the old Mayday processions. Jack-in-the-Green was a prominent figure is these parades. But strangely in this song he is definitely meant to be food. Here are the relevant words of the verse:

"This is the way we bake Jack-in-the-Green...
On a cold and frosty May morning."[142]

Now we come to the last verse. This is about Morris dance, an activity still associated with May Day. Even now

---

139 Ibid, 1984:54.
140 Ibid, 1984:54.
141 Ibid, 1984:54.

Morris dancers perform around the maypole. Here is the appropriate verse:

> *"This is the way we Morris Dance…*
> *On a cold and frosty May morning."*[143]

The Maypoles stood throughout England until 1644 CE, where they were banned throughout England and Wales by the Puritans. They stayed forbidden until the Restoration, when the newly returned king, Charles II revived this important part of England's heritage. They are still a popular feature of Mayday today.

---

[142] Ibid, 1984:54.
[143] Ibid, 1984:54.

SUMMER SOLSTICE

The summer solstice or midsummer's eve was dedicated to the Norse and Germanic god Baldur. This day was the day in which Baldur was killed in mistake by his brother Hodur and had to go down into the land of Hel. Midsummer Day was changed from the Solstice of the 21st and instead of honouring Baldur it was moved three days to June 24th and became the Feast of the Nativity of St. John the Baptist. St John the Baptist died in c. 30 CE. His birthday fell on 24th June six months after the birth of Christ on December 25th. A popular saint, he had at least 496 churches dedicated to him.

The summer solstice is the longest day of the year and the custom was for people to light bonfires to celebrate it. The fire was always circled clockwise. This simulated the path of the sun which rises in the east and sets in the west. Here is an eye witness account of the Midsummer bonfires in 1792 CE in Ireland. It appeared in the *Gentleman's Magazine* of February 1795 CE:

> "At the house where I was entertained it was told me that we should see at midnight the most singular sight in Ireland, which was the lighting of Fires in honour of the Sun. Accordingly, exactly at midnight, the Fires began to appear; and, taking advantage of going up to the leads of the house, which had a widely extended view, I saw on a radius of thirty miles all around the Fires burning on every eminence which the country afforded. I had a farther satisfaction in learning, from an undoubted authority, that the people danced round the Fires, and at the close went through these fires, and made their sons and daughters together with their cattle pass through the Fire; and the whole was conducted with religious solemnity."[144]

That description of a Midsummer bonfire ceremony certainly sounds more like an ancient Pagan rite than a

---

[144] Dictionary of Faiths and Folklore, Hazlitt, 1995:348.

Christian festival. It is even dedicated to the Sun. The jumping through flames also appears to have been a form of pagan cleansing, a homage to the sun, on the longest day of the year.

In another ancient ceremony held on Midsummer Eve, there would be a candlelight procession. The traditional chant uttered during this rite was:

> *"Green is Gold*
> *Fire is Wet*
> *Future's Told*
> *Dragon's Met"*[145]

This is an archaic riddle, creating many questions. When is the colour green gold? This happens at the Spring. Here new leaves shoot up after the dead of the winter. The earth awakens. These new green shoots look gold. Thus this is the time of the year when green looks gold.

The second line states that fire is wet. Now here you have two of the main customs of Midsummer Eve, the bonfire and divination. This is combined in an old tradition called the *'wet fire ritual'*. This is a predictive ceremony. People gather near a pond or lake. They each have a lighted candle. These candles are placed in stiff boats made of paper and floated on the water. Wishes are written on notes placed in the paper boats or on the boats themselves. Now comes the test whether this wish will come true. If the wish and the candle reach the other side of the pond, the request will come to pass. But if the flames get snuffed out in the wind or the boat sinks, then the wish will not be granted. A variation of this traditional ceremony is carried out in seaside towns. Here flaming torches are thrown into the sea. The ritual brings good luck for all the townspeople in the coming year.

Now we have the third line of the riddle. Fortune's told. This is about the common practice of augury at the solstice. Many games of clairvoyance where held on this day. Many of these games used the plant St John's Wort. This is appropriate as Midsummer's Eve was associated with St. John the Baptist. The plant was used to test the strength of love. If the leaves of the plant do not wilt by the end of the day's events, the love will endure. The flower would be taken

---

[145] Medieval Holidays and Festivals, Cosman, 1984:58.

home and kept overnight. This was a stronger test of the power of the love affair. If the herb is still fresh the love will be vigorous, continuous and long lasting. But it the piece of St John's Wort is droopy or wilting, or even worse dead, the duration of the romance is limited.

The last line of the riddle is dragon's met. This is a day for those ancient plays of Mumming. Here people dress up and re-enact traditional tales and folklore. A favourite of Mumming in Midsummer is the story of St George and the Dragon. This is where the English hero and patron saint, St George 'kills' the 'dragon', or large representation of the dragon.

Although there are many traditions concerning this day, this ancient verse sums up the importance of Midsummer and keeps the old Pagan rituals alive.

YULE

Yule was dedicated to the Saxon gods Thor, the god of thunder and Freyr, the god of sunshine and warm showers and a fertility god. Yule began on the longest night of the year, the winter solstice, which was called Mother Night. This was a period of feasting and rejoicing, for now the sun would return and days get longer. In fact it was called Yule, meaning *'wheel'* for the sun was said to represent a wheel rapidly revolving around the sky.

There was a custom popular in England, Germany and on the banks of the Moselle. People would assemble at Yule on a mountain. They would set fire to a huge wooden wheel twined with straw. This flaming wheel would roll down in hill to land in some water, with a spurt of steam. Fire of course was symbolic of Thor. Here is a verse from Naogeorgus describing the ceremony:

> *"Some get a rotten Wheele, all worn and cast aside,*
> *Which, covered round about with strawe and tow, they closely hide;*
> *And caryed to some mountain top, being all with fire light,*
> *They hurle it down with violence, when darke appears the night;*
> *Resembling much the sunne, that from the heavens down should fal,*
> *A strange and monstrous sight it seems, and fearful to them all;*
> *But they suppose their mischiefs are all likewise throwne to hell,*
> *And that from harmes and dangers now, in safetie here they dwell."*[146]

This connection between Yule, Christmas and Thor has survived in some Scandinavian customs. In Sweden biscuits shaped like a goat are served throughout the Christmas feast. The goat was especially sacred to Thor. This is echoed

---

[146] The Norsemen (Myths and Legends), Guerber, 1994:94.

in the practice of goat shaped straw dollies as part of the Swedish Christmas decorations. Thor's goats are evident in the ritual in Norway and Denmark of the Julebukk or *'Christmas Buck'*. This is a children's game in which goat masked boys are rewarded with treats as in the American custom of *'trick or treat'*, on Halloween. In these two countries there was a ancient belief that Thor brought all presents in his goat wagon. Thor traditionally drove a chariot that was pulled by two goats.

Boars were associated with the god Freyr. He rode astride the animal or harnessed it to his golden chariot. This chariot contained the fruits and flowers of the earth, which were lavishly sprinkled over the earth. Interestingly the boar is supposed to have taught man how to plough by tearing up the ground with his sharp tusk. Freyr is therefore god of fertility and agriculture.

This is symbolised in the boar's head that was traditionally placed on the table at Yule. Boar's meat was also eaten. This beast's head would be decked with Laurel and rosemary and carried on to the banqueting table with great ceremony. Here is the *Boars Head Carol*, from Queens College, Oxford:

> *"The Boar's Head in hand bear I*
> *Bedeck'd with bays and rosemary*
> *And I pray you, may masters, be merry."*

In the college this head is carried on a silver platter dated from 1668 CE. The head is ornately decorated with fruit. The singers of the carol receive pieces of the adornment of the boar's head. This head was massive, in 1883 CE, it weighed 65 pounds.

In King's *Art of Cookery* there is the following old recipe for Boars Head at Yule:

> *"At Christmas time-*
> *Then if you wou'd send up the brawne's head,*
> *Sweet rosemary and bays around it spread:*
> *His foaming tusks let some large pippin grace,*
> *Or, 'midst these thundring spears an orange place;*
> *Sauce, like himself, offensive to its foes,*
> *The roguish mustard, dang'rous to the nose.*
> *Sack, and the well-spic'd Hippocras the wine,*
> *Wassail the bowl with the antient ribbands fine,*

Porridge with plumbs, and turkeys with the chine."[147]

There were rituals attached to this boars head. It was called *'the boar of atonement'*. The father of the family would lay his hand on the dish and swear an oath to be faithful to his family. The boars head was sacred. It could only be carved by someone without blemish. This holiness of the boars head was the reason why it appeared on the helmets of Northern Kings and heroes. It symbolised the utmost bravery.

But perhaps the most famous Yule custom is that of the Yule log. This was a massive log that burnt threw out the whole night. Later this was altered to being kept lit through the twelve days of Christmas. If it went out it would be a very bad omen. This enormous log burning in the grate has become a well loved symbol of Christmas. It was normally of well seasoned oak. This log was decorated with ribbons and taken home from the woods in triumph on Christmas Eve. It was the custom to doff your hat when seeing this bedecked log being brought home. This festival was known in Tuscany as *Festa le Ceppo*, the Festival of the Log. In Germany it was the Christbrand or Christklotz. Here are Robert's Herrick's instructions of 1648 CE concerning the Yule Log:

> *"With the last year's brand,*
> *Light the new block, and*
> *For good success in his spending*
> *On your psaltries play*
> *That sweet luck may*
> *Come while the log is a-tending".*[148]

What Herrick is referring to is the practice of the collection of the Yule log ashes. These were carefully preserved and used to ignite the next year's log.

It is interesting that one of our best loved and most popular festivals, Christmas developed from the earlier custom of giving homage to the ancient Norse gods of Thor and Freyr.

---

[147] Dictionary of Faiths and Folklore, Hazlitt, 1995:60.
[148] Observations on Popular Antiquities, Brand, 1888:249

BIBLIOGRAPHY

Asser, John & Simon Keynes (trans) (1984) *Alfred the Great, Asser's Life of King Alfred and Other Contemporary Sources*. London, Penguin Classics

Baker, Margaret (1994) *Discovering Christmas Customs and Folklore*. Essex, Shire Publications

Bernstein, Melissa (2004) *The Electronic Sermo Lupi ad Anglos*. http://english3.fsu.edu/~wulfstan/noframes.html

Boenig, Robert (2001) *Anglo-Saxon Spirituality: Selected Writings*. New Jersey, Paulist Press

Borges, Jorge Luis (1987) *The Book of Imaginary Beings*. London, Penguin

Boyce, Mary (ed, trans) (1984) *Textual Sources for the Study of Zoroastrianism*. Chicago, University of Chicago Press

Brand, John (2003) *Observations on Popular Antiquities 1888 Part 1*. Kessinger Publishing LLC

Branston, Brian (1993) *The Lost Gods of England*. London, Constable

----------- (1955) *Gods of the North*. London, Thames and Hudson

Brewer, Ebenezer Cobham (1898) *Brewer's Dictionary of Phrase and Fable*, www.bartleby.com

Bickerman, E.J. (1968) *Chronology of the Ancient World*. New York, Cornell University Press

Cameron, Kenneth (1996) *English Place Names*, new revised edition. London, B.T. Batsford Ltd

Carnoy, Albert (1955) *Dictionnaire Etymologique du Proto-Indo-Européen*. Bibliothèque du Muséon 39. Louvain: Publications Universitaires, Institut Orientaliste

Chance, Jane (2004) *Tolkien and the Invention of Myth: A Reader*. Kentucky, University of Kentucky Press

Chevalier, Jean & Alain Gheerbrant & John Buchanan-Brown (trans) (1996) *The Penguin Dictionary of Symbols*. London, Penguin

Cooper, J.C. (1993) *Brewer's Book of Myth and Legend*. London, Cassell

Cosman, Madeleine Pelner (1984) *Medieval Holidays and Festivals*. London, Piatkus

Crossley-Holland, Kevin (1993) *The Penguin Book of Norse Myths*. London, Penguin

---------- (1982) *The Anglo-Saxon World* (includes translation of Beowulf). Oxford, Oxford University Press

Curtis, Vesta Sarkhosh (1993) *Persian Myths*. London, British Museum Press

De Vries, Jan (1963) *Heroic Song and Heroic Legend*. Oxford, Oxford University Press

Dronke, Ursula (trans) (1969) *The Poetic Edda*. Oxford, Clarendon Press

Dumezil, Georges (1977) *Gods of the Ancient Northmen*. California, University of California Press

Ebbutt, M.I. (1994) *Myths and Legends of the British*. London, Senate

Eliade, Mircea (1981) *A History of Religious Ideas*, Volumes I & 2. Chicago, University of Chicago Press

Ellis, Peter Berresford (1993) *Dictionary of Celtic Mythology*. London, Constable

Evans, Ivor H. (1993) *The Wordsworth Dictionary of Phrase and Fable*. Ware, Wordsworth Reference

Farmer, David Hugh (1980) *The Oxford Dictionary of Saints*. Oxford, Oxford University Press

Fisher, Douglas John (1989) *The Anglo-Saxon Age c.400-1042*. Lancaster, Gazelle Book Services

Frazer, Sir James (1993) *The Golden Bough*. London, Wordsworth

Garmonsway, G.N. (trans, ed) (1975) *The Anglo-Saxon Chronicle*. Canada, J.M. Dent & Sons Ltd

Grant, John (2002) *An Introduction to Viking Mythology*. New Jersey, Chartwell Books

Grant, Michael & John Hazel (2002) *Who's Who in Classical Mythology*. London, Routledge

Griffiths, Bill (1996) *Aspects of Anglo Saxon Magic*. Norfolk, Anglo-Saxon Books

Grimal, Pierre (1969) *Larousse World Mythology*. London, Hamlyn Publishing Group

Guerber, H.A. (1994) *Greece and Rome (Myths and Legends)*. London, Senate

---------- (1994) *Myths and Legends of the Middle Ages*. London, Dover

---------- (1994) *The Norsemen (Myths and Legends)*. London, Senate

Hadley, Dawn M. (2006) *The Vikings in England: Settlement, Society and Culture.* Manchester, Manchester University Press

Hall, John R Clark (trans) & C.L. Wrenn (intr) (1950) *Beowulf and the Finnesburg Fragment.* London, Allen & Unwin

Hazlitt, W.C. (1995) *Dictionary of Faiths and Folklore.* London, Bracken

Hinnells, John R. (1985) *Persian Mythology.* Feltham, Newnes.

Hole, Christina (1995) *Dictionary of British Folk Customs.* Oxford, Helicon

Hooker, Sir William Jackson (1811) *Journal of a Tour in Iceland in the Summer of 1809.* Yarmouth, J. Keymer

Howe, George & G.A. Harrer (1996) *A Handbook of Classical Mythology.* Hertfordshire, Oracle

Jones, Alison (1995) *Larousse Dictionary of World Folklore.* Edinburgh, Larousse

Jones, Gwyn (1984) *A History of the Vikings.* Oxford, Oxford University Press

Jonson, Ben & W. Gifford (intro) (2004) *Every Man Out of His Humour, Cynthia's Revels and The Poetaster: The Works of Ben Jonson Part Two.* Kessinger Publishing LLC

Jordan, Michael (1995) *Myths of the World.* London, Kyle Cathie

---------- (1994) *The Encyclopaedia of Gods.* London, Kyle Cathie

Kendrick, T.D. (1968) *A History of the Vikings.* London, Frank Cass & Co. Ltd

Knappert, Jan (1995) *Indian Mythology.* London, Harper Collins

Licht, Hans (1994) *Sexual Life in Ancient Greece.* London, Constable & Co

MacCulloch, J.A. (1993) *The Celtic and Scandinavian Religions.* London, Constable

Magnusson, Magnus & Hermann Palsson (trans) (1966) *King Harald's Saga.* London, Penguin Classics

---------- (trans) (1968) *The Vinland Sagas, the Norse Discovery of America.* London, Penguin

Matthews, John & Caitlin (1995) *British and Irish Mythology.* Cheshire, Diamond Books

Muller, C.F. (1855) *Geograph Graeci Minores.* Paris, Institute of French Typography

No Author (1996) *Dictionary of Saints*. Leicester, Brockhampton Press

Orchard, Andy (1997) *Dictionary of Norse Myth and Legend*. London, Cassell

Ovid, & John Dryden & Alexander Pope & other eminent hands (trans) (1717) *Metamorphoses*. www.sacred-texts.com

Palgrave, Francis (1995) *A History of the Anglo-Saxons*. London, Senate

Palsson, Herman (trans) (1971) *Hrafnkel's Saga and Other Icelandic Stories*. London, Penguin

Palsson, Hermann & Paul Edwards (trans) (1978) *Egil's Saga*. London, Penguin Books

Pliny the Elder & John F Healy (trans) (1991) *Natural History: A Selection*. London, Penguin

Pollington, Stephen (2000) *Leechcraft: Early English Charms Plantlore and Healing*. Norfolk, Anglo-Saxon Books

Purser, John (1993) *Scotland's Music: A History of the Traditional and Classical Music of Scotland from Earliest Times to the Present Day*. London, Trafalgar Square

Richards, Julian D. (2004) *Viking Age England*. Exeter, NPI Media Group Ltd

Rolleston, T.W. (1990) *Celtic Myths and Legends*. London, Dover

Room, Adrian (1993) *Brewers Dictionary of Names*. London, Cassell.

Sawyer, Prof. P.H. (1982) *Kings and Vikings: Scandinavia and Europe AD 700-1100*. London, Methuen Young Books

----------- (1971) *The Age of the Vikings*. London, Edward Arnold Ltd

Scott, A.F. (1979) *The Saxon Age, Commentaries of an Era*. London, Croom Helm

Scott, George Riley (1995) *A History of Torture*. Merchant Book Company Limited

Speake, Graham (ed) (1995) *Dictionary of Ancient History*. London, Puffin

Steel, Duncan (1999) *Marking Time: The Epic Quest to Invent the Perfect Calendar*. New Jersey, John Wiley & Sons

Stephenson, Joseph (1996) *A History of the Kings of England by Florence of Worcester*. Felinfach, Llanerch Publishers

Stow, John & Henry Morley (2007) *A Survey of London*. Fairford, Echo Library

Sykes, Egerton & Alan Kendall (1993) *Who's Who in Non-Classical Mythology*. Oxford, Oxford University Press

Thorpe, Benjamin (ed) (2004) *Ancient Laws and Institutes of England*. London, Lawbook Exchange Ltd

Tolley, Clive (2009) *Shamanism in Norse Myth and Magic*. Helsinki, Academia Scientiarum Fennica

Turnville-Petre, E.O.G. (1975) *Myth and Religion of the North*. London, Weidnefeld & Nicolson

Tusser, Thomas (1984) *Five Hundred Points of Good Husbandry*. Oxford, Oxford University Press

Wedeck, H.E. (1994) *A Dictionary of Aphrodisiacs*. London, Bracken Books

Whaling, Frank (1994) *Larousse Dictionary of Beliefs and Religions*. London, Larousse

Whitelock, Dorothy (1979) *English Historical Documents 500-1042* vol 1. London, Routledge

Whitlock, Ralph (1978) *A Calendar of Country Customs*. London, Batsford

Young, Jean I. (1964) *The Prose Edda of Snorri Sturluson*. New Jersey, University of California

INDEX

A

Abundia, 177
Acheron, River, 104
Adam of Bremen, 55, 57, 69
Adonis, 131, 184
Aecerbot, 36
Aegir, 191
Aesir, 57, 92, 96, 105, 114, 126, 129, 159, 176, 181, 188, 191, 193
Aethelstan, King, 40, 41, 42
Afra-Fasti, 72
Agathemenus, 19
Ahura Mazda, 81
Alfablot, 90
Alfheim, 88, 89, 96
Alfred, King, 28, 38
Allsvin, 85
Alsvid, 123
Alsvider, 85
Al-Tartushi, 47
Althjof, 90
Amalthea, 163
Anaximander, 19
Anaximenes, 19
Andhrimnir, 101
Anglo-Saxon Chronicle, 66, 72, 118, 155, 160
Angra Mainyu, 81
Angrboda, 104, 190
Annar, 86
Aphrodite, 131
Apollo, 125, 136, 137, 148
Armageddon, 58, 108, 111, 114, 116, 194
Artemis, 136, 137
Arvak, 123
Arvakr, 85

Asgard, 57, 91, 92, 94, 96, 105, 111, 117, 126, 129, 130, 140, 168, 176, 177, 178, 184, 190, 194
Ask, 91
Athena, 35, 113
Attila, 141
Aud, 48, 86
Audhumla, 81
Augustus, Emperor, 23
Aurgelmir, 80, *See* Ymir

B

Baal, 184
Bald's Leechbook, 37
Baldur, 92, 96, 102, 117, 125, 126, 127, 128, 129, 130, 131, 132, 150, 190, 191, 207
Bede, 198, 199, 200
Beldeg, 159
Beowulf, 27, 28, 29, 30, 31, 32, 34, 35, 63
Bergelmir, 81, 82, 83
Bestla, 81
Bifrost, 94, 95, 111
Bil, 85, 134
Bilfur, 90
Bolthorn, 81
Bombor, 90
Bor, 81, 82, 83, 90, 91
Bragi, 150
Brahma, 134
Breidablik, 92, 126
Brian Boru, King, 175
Brihaspati, 162
Brimir, 117

Brisingamen, 186
Brock, 186
Buri, 81
Byleist, 188, 189

C

Cadmus, 35
Cain, 28, 134, 156
Cambridge MS 41, 37
Canis Major, 18
Canute, King, 28, 72, 73
Cerberus, 102
Charon, 104
Cheru, 141
Christ, 38, 39, 42, 48, 62, 73,
    119, 132, 157, 160, 162,
    170, 171, 172, 174, 201,
    207
Constantine, Emperor, 23
Copernicus, 19
Cotton MS Caligula A.vii., 36,
    37
Cronos, 188

D

Dagda, 167
Dain, 57, 90
Dark Elves, 86, 96
Day, 86
De Temporum Ratione, 198,
    199
Dellinger, 86
Demeter, 96
Deskford Carnyx, 112
Dian Cecht, 146
Diomedes, 153
Dionysus, 113, 163
Domaldi, King, 52
Donar, 161
Dragon, 30, 32, 35, 36, 57,
    112, 118, 127, 167, 209
Draupnir, 88, 127, 129, 131,
    154, 170
Dream of the Rood, 132
Droma, 104, 144

Duneyr, 57
Durathror, 57
Durin, 90
Dvalin, 57, 90, 170
Dwarves, 83, 86, 88, 90, 91,
    94, 96, 114, 141, 144, 154,
    186, 187
Dyeus, 140, 167

E

Einherjar, 58, 98, 114, 115,
    148
Einmyria, 189
Eira, 180
Eirik's Saga, 171
Eisa, 189
Eldhrimnir, 101
Elivager, 79
Elves, 28, 38, 88, 90, 94, 96,
    104, 191
Elvidnir, 105
Embla, 91
Endymion, 134, 137, 138
Eostre, 199
Epona, 44
Erda, 161
Ethelred the Redeless, King,
    67
Eyrbyggja Saga, 48
Eysteinn Beli, King, 63

F

Farbauti, 188, 189
Fenrir, 104, 105, 110, 111,
    114, 115, 144, 190
Fensalir, 177
Fimbulthul, River, 79
Fimbulvetr, 108, 110
Finn, 27, 71
Fiorgyn, 150
Fjalar, 65, 114
Fjorgvin, 176
Fjorm, River, 79
Flateyjarbok, 67, 190
Folkvangar, 184

Foresti, 92
Freki, 151, 153
Freya, 52, 183, 184, 185, 186, 187, 191
Freyr, 51, 52, 55, 62, 114, 115, 170, 184, 186, 187, 198, 210, 211, 212
Fricco, 55, 62, *See* Freyr
Friday, 16, 21, 44, 46, 176
Frigg, 21, 44, 46, 125, 126, 127, 129, 131, 140, 150, 176, 177, 178, 179, 180, 183, 186
Fulla, 129, 177

G

Galdr, 159
Gandalf, 90
Garm, 101, 111, 114, 115
Gauka-Thorir, 72
Gautreks Saga, 53
Gayomart, 81
Geats, 27, 30, 34
Gefjon, 180, 181, 182
Geri, 151, 153
Gesta Danorum, 68
Gesta Hammaburgensis, 69
Giallar, 94
Gimle, 94, 117, 149
Ginnungagap, 77, 78, 79, 80, 83
Gjoll, 65, 79, 102, 104, 112, 129
Gladsheim, 92
Gleipnir, 105, 144
Glen, 123
Glitnir, 92
Glut, 189
Gna, 178
Gnipahellir, 101
Goinn, 118
Götaland, 30
Gram, King, 65
Greek Magical Papyri, 138
Grendel, 28, 29, 30, 32, 35
Grid, 115, 150

Grim, 45, 148
Groa, 170
Gullinbursti, 186
Gullinkambi, 65, 114
Gungnir, 88, 114, 154, 157, 170
Gunnar Helming, 62
Gunnlod, 150
Gunnthra, River, 79
Gylfi, King, 181, 182

H

Hades, 28, 65, 102, 104, 131, 136, 147
Hallfred, 68
Haoma, 135, 136
Harley MS 585, 38
Hathor, 82
Hati, 85, 87, 110
Hauksbok, 119
Heidrun, 101
Heimdall, 92, 93, 94, 96, 112, 115
Hel, 57, 65, 79, 80, 96, 98, 101, 102, 103, 104, 105, 107, 111, 114, 115, 117, 127, 129, 130, 131, 149, 190, 201, 207
Helblindi, 148, 188, 189
Helgi the Lean, 48
Helios, 123, 124, 125, 137
Hengest, 27, 160
Hercules, 35, 154
Hermod, 65, 96, 102, 127, 129, 150
Hermundurii, 142
Herodotus, 19
Hildisvin, 186
Himinbjorg, 92
Hlidskialf, 94, 176
Hlidskjalf, 150
Hlin, 177
Hod, 117, 190, *See* Hodur
Hoddmfmir's Wood, 119
Hodur, 126, 127, 130, 131, 190, 207

Homer, 16, 17
Horsa, King, 160
Hreasvelgr, 86
Hretha, 199
Hrimfaxi, 86
Hriod, River, 79
Hrothgar, King, 27, 28, 29, 30
Hrungnir, 168
Hrym, 111
Hugin, 151, 152
Huiki, 85
Hvergelmir, 57, 79, 118
Hygelac, King, 27
Hymir, 140

I

Iarn-greiper, 167
Ibn Fadlan, 64, 65
Ibn Rustah, 55, 64
Idavoll, 117, 130
Indra, 167
Iping, 90

J

Jarnsaxa, 168
Jaroslav, King, 72
Jord, 86, 150, 161, 167, 176
Jormungand, 104, 105, 190
Josephus, Flavius, 15
Jotunheim, 82, 90, 96, 104, 105
Jove, 55, 147, 161, *See* Jupiter
Jupiter, 21, 22, 55, 161, 162, 167

K

Kelpie, 153
Ketill, 48
Krakumal, 118
Kvasir, 193
Kybele, 184

L

Ladon, 35
Laeding, 104, 144
Landnamabok, 170
Laufey, 188, 189
Laws of Cnut, 73
Lay of Sigdrifa, 144
Lif, 119
Lofn, 180
Lofthrasir, 119
Lokasenna, 190
Loki, 21, 104, 105, 106, 111, 114, 115, 126, 127, 130, 131, 144, 153, 162, 170, 187, 188, 189, 190, 191, 192, 193, 194
Loridi, 170
Lucifer, 188, 189
Luna, 137

M

Magni, 117, 130, 168
Managarm, 85
Mani, 83, 85, 110, 133, 134, 136, 137
Mars, 21, 22, 55, 140
Maypole, 203, 204
Megin-gjord, 167
Mercury, 21, 22, 147
Midgard, 57, 85, 91, 92, 94, 96, 104, 110, 111, 114, 115, 167, 190
Mimir, 113, 157, 159
Mithra, 124
Mithras, 123
Mjodvitnir, 90
Mjollnir, 88, 130, 162, 164, 165, 167, 191
Modgud, 102, 104, 129
Modi, 117, 130, 168
Modsognir, 90
Monday, 16, 21, 133, 134, 182, 183
Moon, 21, 22, 82, 85, 86, 123, 133, 134, 135

Mornir, 71
MS Cotton Julius C2, 37
MS Royal 12.D, xvii, 38
Mundilfari, 83, 123
Munin, 151, 152
Muses, 96
Muspell, 78, 79, 80, 83, 96,
    111, 112, 116, 123

N

Naglfar, 111
Naglfari, 86
Nain, 90
Nanna, 127, 129, 131
Nar, 90
Narfi, 85, 193
Narve, 190
Nastrand, 117
Natural History, 164
Necromancy, 28
Nerthus, 186
New Testament, 108, 113,
    116
Nidafjoll, 117
Nidavellir, 96
Nidhogg, 57, 112, 118
Niflheim, 57, 78, 79, 80, 96,
    101, 102, 105
Niflhel, 101, 149
Njord, 71
Nori, 90
Norns, 58, 195
Nott, 85
Nuada, 145
Nuit, 81
Nundinae, 15

O

Oceanus, 79, 124
Odin, 2, 27, 38, 45, 46, 51,
    52, 53, 54, 57, 58, 62, 63,
    81, 82, 86, 88, 91, 92, 94,
    96, 98, 101, 113, 114, 115,
    117, 119, 125, 126, 127,
    129, 130, 131, 140, 146,
    147, 148, 149, 150, 151,
    153, 154, 156, 157, 158,
    159, 160, 161, 167, 170,
    175, 176, 177, 178, 181,
    184, 187, 189, 190, 191,
    193, 198, 199, 201
Offa, King, 27, 45, 160
Oin, 90
Okolnir, 117
Olaf Haraldson, King, 70
Olaf Tryggvason, King, 62,
    66, 68, 69, 70, 174
Olaus Magnus, 202
Old Testament, 17, 113
Olympus, 96, 148
Onar, 90
Orion, 18, 177
Ostara, 199
Ovid, 77, 78, 80

P

Penda, King, 160
Persephone, 96
Pliny, 164

R

Ra, 123
Ragnarok, 58, 65, 94, 98,
    102, 105, 108, 109, 110,
    113, 116, 117, 119, 130,
    134, 148, 150, 167, 194
Ragnars Lodbrokar's Saga, 63
Ratatosk, 57
Renir, 159
Rerir, King, 178
Revelations, 108, 116, 154
Rig Veda, 114
Rind, 130, 150, 198
Roskva, 162, 163

S

Sabbath, 15, 16, 22, 123,
    133, 134
Saeming, 160

Saga, 70, 150, 171
Saint Anskar, 55
Saint Augustine, 10
Saint Columba, 171
Saint George, 36, 209
Saint Gertrude, 187
Saint Hubert, 201
Saint James, 203
Saint John, 207, 208
Saint Michael, 36, 142
Saint Olaf, 60, 70, 73
Saint Patrick, 171
Saint Valentine, 94, 198
Sataere, 21, 188
Satan, 36, 194
Saturday, 16, 21, 22, 188
Saturn, 21, 22, 188
Saxnot, 140, 175
Saxo Grammatiicus, 68
Seahrimnir, 101
Seamund's Edda, 80, 189
Seidr, 159
Selene, 137, 138, 139
Sermon of the Wolf, 66
Shamash, 123
Short Voluspa, 190
Shu, 81
Sibilja, 63
Sif, 169, 170
Sigi, 159, 178
Sigrid, Queen, 69
Sigyn, 188, 190, 194
Sindri, 117, 154, 164
Sinmora, 80
Skadi, 71, 194
Skidbladnir, 88, 170
Skinfaxi, 86
Skinir, 115
Skirnir, 104
Skjold, 159
Skoll, 85, 87, 110
Skuld, 58
Sleipnir, 127, 153, 154, 157, 190
Slid, River, 79
Snorri Sturluson, 52, 57, 60, 63, 68, 70, 77, 78, 79, 80,

91, 92, 95, 98, 116, 118, 123, 126, 129, 130, 134, 140, 145, 148, 149, 151, 153, 157, 159, 161, 168, 176, 177, 178, 180, 181, 184, 188, 200
Snotra, 180
Sokkvabekk, 150
Sol, 83, 110, 123, 125, 133, 136
Solomon and Saturn, 147, 161, 176
Soma, 134, 135
Sophocles, 41
Starkad, 53, 54
Steinunn, 172, 174
Story of Volsi, 70
Styx, River, 104
Suabian, 142
Sucellus, 167
Sun, 21, 22, 86, 96, 123, 135, 136, 207, 208
Surt, 79, 80, 111, 114, 115, 116, 130
Surya, 124
Sutton Hoo, 28, 150
Svadilfari, 153, 190
Svartalfheim, 86, 88, 96, 97, 104
Sven Forkbeard, 66, 67, 69
Svol, River, 79
Sylg, River, 79
Syn, 180

T

Tacitus, 46, 186
Tale of Hadding, 65
Tammuz, 184
Thangbrand, 172, 174
The Deluding of Gylfi, 58
The Prose Edda, 52, 57, 77, 79, 80, 91, 92, 95, 98, 116, 118, 123, 126, 129, 130, 134, 140, 145, 149, 151, 159, 161, 168, 176, 181, 184, 188, 200

Thialfi, 162, 163
Thor, 21, 44, 45, 48, 49, 53, 55, 60, 62, 67, 68, 88, 115, 117, 127, 130, 150, 161, 162, 163, 164, 165, 166, 167, 168, 170, 171, 172, 174, 175, 176, 191, 193, 198, 210, 212
Thorhall the Hunter, 171, 172
Thorin, 90
Thorkell the Tall, 51
Thormod, 71
Thorolf Mostrarskegg, 62
Thrudgelmir, 80
Thunor, 44, 45, 140, 161, 175, *See* Thor
Thursday, 16, 21, 44, 45, 150, 161, 162
Thyri, 69
Tiw, 21, 44, 140
Tomair, 175
Travel Book of Ibrahim ibn Jakub, 47
Tuatha De Danann, 145
Tuesday, 16, 21, 44, 133, 140, 150
Tyr, 53, 114, 115, 140, 141, 142, 143, 144, 145, 146, 150, 175

U

Ull, 200, 201
Urd, 58
Utgard, 96
Utgard-Loki, 96

V

Vajra, 167
Valaskjalf, 94
Valhalla, 58, 60, 61, 65, 66, 96, 98, 99, 101, 102, 105, 110, 111, 114, 115, 147, 148, 161, 168, 191

Vali, 94, 117, 130, 150, 190, 193, 198
Valkyries, 98
Vanaheim, 96
Vanir, 96
Vara, 180
Vasud, 86
Ve, 81, 82, 91, 177
Vedrfolnir, 57
Vegdeg, 159
Venus, 21, 22, 176
Verdandi, 58
Vetrlidi, 172
Vid, River, 79
Vidfinn, 134
Vidofnir, 65
Vidor, 115, 117, 130, 150
Vig, 90
Viga-Glums Saga, 51
Vigrid, 111
Vikar, King, 53, 54
Vili, 81, 82, 91, 177
Vindaul, 86
Vingolf, 92, 148, 149
Vingull, 71
Vinndalf, 90
Virgin Mary, 136, 187, 198
Vitellius, 141
Vjofn, 180
Volsung, 178
Voluspa bin Skamma, 119
Vor, 180

W

Wednesday, 16, 21, 44, 147
Wiglaf, 32, 34
Wild Hunt, 154, 155, 156
Woden, 21, 27, 38, 39, 44, 45, 55, 62, 140, 147, 160, 175
Wuffings, 28
Wulfings, 28
Wulfstan, Archbishop, 66

Y

Yasha 9, 135
Yggdrasil, 57, 58, 59, 65, 79, 88, 98, 113, 114, 115, 118, 156, 157
Ylg, River, 79

Ymir, 80, 81, 82, 83, 86, 90, 91
Yngvi, 160

Z

Zeus, 96, 131, 137, 163

Ingram Content Group UK Ltd.
Milton Keynes UK
UKHW021808220523
422165UK00007B/105

9 781905 297443